Stone-Tree Houses of Texas
Charles Garrett

For Ron
Charlie

ABOUT THE AUTHOR

West Texas native Charlie Garrett moved to Austin in the late 1960s and to the Lake Travis area in the 1980s, where he worked in water utility operations and management. He now pursues long-term retirement projects, book publishing and travels.

Stone-Tree Houses of Texas

Copyright © 2012

by Charles G. Garrett- All Rights Reserved
No part of this book may be reproduced in any form or by any electronic or mechanical means including information storage and retrieval systems without permission in writing from the publisher, except by a reviewer who may quote brief passages in a review.
Published by **Rockstone Press**
4020 High Rim Road, Spicewood, TX, 78669

Printed In China

ISBN-13: 978-0-9847694-1-4

ISBN-10: 0984769412

All photos not otherwise credited are by Charles Garrett

Edited by Beverly Walker

Book design, graphics, and layout by Timothy John Davis

Cover Photos: The Pressley House, pg. 172; Young's Service Station, pg. 103

Dedicated to my mother

LENORA JEAN THOMPSON GARRETT

Table of Contents

Acknowledgements	VI
About the book	VII
About Scott Singleton	VII
Map: Geology of Texas	VIII
Map: Distribution of Stone-Tree Houses	IX

Northwestern/Caprock Region — 1

Alanreed	Bruce Nursery	3
Amarillo	McCollum House	10
	Heath House	15
Canyon	Buffalo Courts	19
Matador	Bob's Cook Shack	27
Abernathy	Shadden House	31
	Bill Garrett, Stonemason	34
	Anderson House	37
Anton	Brazil House	41
Idalou	Knoles House	43
Lubbock	Fisher / Hufstedler House	47
	Brunson House	49
Acuff	Moore House	53
Rotan	Vittitow House	57
Snyder	King House	63

Western Region — 65

Alpine	Walker House	66
Castolon	Dorgan House	69

North Central Region — 73

Decatur	Texas Tourist Camp	75
Jacksboro	Nash House	79
Fort Worth	Williams House	81
	Schnieder / Burger House	85
	O.D. Stevens House	87
	Stevens Commercial Building	91
Colleyville	Black House	93
	Walter Reynolds, Stonemason	95
Gordon	Ringo House	97
Abilene	Shoemaker House	99
Glen Rose	Sycamore Grove/Young's Service Station	103
	Historic Town Square	105
	Milling Sanitarium	106
	Snyder House	106
	Lane's Ford Agency	107
	Fire Station / City Hall	107
	Marsh House	108
	Gresham House	109
	Pruitt House	109
Stephenville	Wolfe Nursery	110
	Latham House	117
Rising Star	City Cannery / City Hall	120
Dublin	Hudson House	123
	Hughes House	127
Bronte	Youngblood House	129
San Angelo	Jennings House	133
	Young House	135
	Ollie Young, Stonemason	136
	Leddy House	138
	Curry House	141
	Curry Wonder Shop	142

Stone-Tree Houses of Texas

Northeastern Region — 147
Tyler	Smith House	149
Rusk	Schochler House	151

South Central Region — 153
Austin	Petrified Forest Lodge	155
Harper	Peril Ranch House	157
Bandera	Frontier Times Museum	159

Southeastern Region — 165
Lufkin	Read House	167
Jasper	Munson / Kinnear House	171
Hoyte	Pressley House	172
Lexington	Hornung House	179
Rockdale	Copeland / Fiesler House	185
	Chamber of Commerce/Coffield House	189
Cooks Point	Chaloupka House	191
	Urbanovsky House	193
	Drgac House	195
	Cooks Point Brethren Church	197
Caldwell	Woodson House	198
	E.K. Treeter, Stonemason	200
	Burleson County Fair Grounds Ticket Office	201
Snook	Elsik House	203
Somerville	Nedbalek House	205
	L.C. Hudson House	207
Brenham	Meyer House	211
	Benjamin Whitmarsh, Stonemason	212
	Public Cannery	215
Columbus	Kerr House	217
Gonzales	Halamicek House	221

Houston	Helweg House	223
Brookshire	Longenbaugh House / Eve's Garden	225
	England House	227
Garwood	Zboril House	229
Huntsville	Willhoite House	231

Southern Region — 235
San Antonio	Nowotny House	236
Seguin	Pape House	243
Adams Gardens	Entry Gates	247
Donna	Cummings House	250

Appendices
Appendix A: *Petrified Wood Colors and Petrification* — 257
Appendix B: *Site Status and Preservation Prospects* — 258
Appendix C: *Anatomy of Fossil Woods and Paleoclimate in the Texas Gulf Coast Tertiary and Cretaceous, Part 2* — 260
Appendix D: *Anatomy of Fossil Woods and Paleoclimate in the Texas Gulf Coast Tertiary and Cretaceous, Part 3* — 262
Appendix E: References and Publications, Scott Singleton — 264
Appendix F: *Specifications: The Hart Shoemaker House* — 266
Appendix G: Tom Garrett, Stonemason — 268

ACKNOWLEDGEMENTS

I wish to gratefully acknowledge the assistance of all the families, homeowners, librarians, historians and elders who made this book possible by inviting me into their homes and archives and museums and sharing their memories. I especially thank those who helped me locate fossil wood structures – I could never have driven down enough dirt roads to find them all myself. An incomplete list of contributors follows. **– Charles Garrett**

Amarillo: Gayle Brown and the Amarillo Public Library; Betty Bustos; the Richardsons; the Tuckers
Canyon: West Texas A&M Alumni Association; WTAMU Library; Warren Stricker and the Panhandle Plains Historical Museum
McLean: Robert Bruce and family
Clarendon: Walt Warner
Matador: Mary Sue Potts; Barbara Armstrong; the Matador Museum
Abernathy: The Shaddens; Tim Hill; Olin Anderson; Don Barron
Anton: The Kristineks
Ida Lou: James Emory
Lubbock: The Hufstedlers; Sally Abbe and the Lubbock City Planning Department
Crosbyton: Crosbyton Museum; Susannah Horn
Acuff: Bud Barnett
Rotan: Odessa Clements
Snyder: Bill King
Abilene: Gary Garson; the Shoemaker family
Alpine: The Woodward Ranch; National Parks Service, Big Bend; Archives of the Big Bend
Hamilton: Agnes Walker
Glen Rose: Dorothy Leach, Somervell County Historical Society
Texarkana: Willena Woodard
Jacksboro: Jacksboro Public Library
Decatur: The Rosendahls
Gordon: Debbie Wheeler and Jon Johnson
Abilene: Stephenville: The Stephenville History Museum; Brenda Hansen; Joyce Whitis; the late Hugh Wolfe; Syl Logan
Mineral Wells: Jim Drews
Rising Star: the Halls
Dublin: Mary Yantis; Dublin Historical Museum; J.W. Davis
Mansfield: Mrs. Tom Jack Hughes
Bronte: The Glenns and Hometown Hardware

San Angelo: Angelo State University-West Texas Collection, Elmo Curry; Don Jennings; the Allens; Jake Young
Cameron: Richard Stone
Fort Worth: Jerre Tracy, Historic Forth Worth, Inc.; Susan Pritchett, Tarrant County Archives
Waxahachie: Frank R. Williams III
Rusk: The Schochlers
Euless: Lori Black Johnson
Austin: Dolph Briscoe Center for American History; Austin History Center; Bob Brinkman and Greg Smith and the Texas Historical Commission; Stan Kosinsky; Zane Morgan; Jim Bigger; Merle Willhoite Conley and Julia Willhoite
Harper: Peggy Bateman and Jimmy Peril
Bandera: Rebecca Norton, Frontier Times Museum
Granite Shoals: Glynis Smith
Marble Falls: Billy Becker
Lufkin: Marty Tatum; Dr. Royce Read; the East Texas Museum
Hoyte: Pauline McDermott
Lexington: the Hoopers and the Browns
Rockdale: Rockdale Chamber of Commerce
Bryan: Patsy Albright
Caldwell: John Treeter; the late Mayor Bernard Rychlik; Debbie Womble; Ann Chapman
Cooks Point: Tracy Wine
Brenham: The Cannery Kitchen; Marty Whitmarsh; Dr. Henry Boehm
Snook: Matt Elsik
Bedford: The Conner brothers
Houston: The Kerrs; Marla Van Overbeke; Betty Glass
Fayetteville: Beatrice Helweg
Brookshire: Anice Devin; Annie Laurie Day and the Denmarks
Garwood: Viola Zboril
San Augustine: El Camino Real de los Tejas National Historic Trail Association

Boerne: The Nowotnys
San Antonio: Carlos Cortez
Harlingen: Ofelia Ashworth; Leo San Pedro
Donna: Donna Hooks Fletcher History Museum; Donna Public Library; the Abregos
Weslaco: The Housleys; Fran Isbell
Edinburg: George Gause, University of Texas Pan America Library
Kingsville: The Nollkampers
Harlingen: Norman Rozeff
Kerrville: Cora Jean Fuller

Enid, Okla.: The Midgley Museum, Enid, Okla.
Holbrook, Ariz.: Petrified Forest National Park
Hawaii: Pam Woodard Tajima
Arizona: Trisha Stanton

About the Book

The intention of this book is to introduce readers to examples of a little known and largely unrecognized vernacular art form created mainly during the 1930s and mainly in Texas: the use of petrified wood, mineral samples and other colorful and unusual stones in a variety of masonry constructions. A few houses constructed with fossil wood have been found in the adjoining border areas of Louisiana and Oklahoma and one or two in other states but all indications are that the epicenter of this phenomenon was Texas.

Perhaps the impetus to build with this type of material reflected a confluence of conditions at the time. Few jobs and low wages during the Great Depression caused skilled workers to seek labor-intensive, long-term projects, including federally funded public works. The development of mechanized equipment such as tractors and winches and trucks made collecting stones easier and public funding for highways had opened up new roads and access to remote locations where these materials were found.

Yet another factor – new discoveries in geology and paleontology and other sciences – encouraged interest in the process of mineralization of primeval trees. It was inherently intriguing that wood turned to stone and it was as well a tangible link to millions of years of history. The northern and western areas of the state were especially affected by the dust bowl conditions of the 1930s; the colorful and unusual appearance of these buildings may have helped alleviate the bleak environment and the rocks were available.

Most of the buildings were private homes, but some were commercial buildings for small businesses and some were WPA-financed public works projects; some were the proud culmination of years of collecting by "rockhounds"; some were reflections of the Arts and Crafts trend toward using natural materials; some reflect the eccentricities and obsessions of the builders. Some have historical markers or are in historic districts and some have been demolished.

Because of the amount of work involved, it is safe to say that those who built stone-tree houses very much wanted them. One of the purposes of this collection is to recognize these unique buildings and raise awareness of their part in the histories of Texas communities as well as to encourage their protection and preservation. An appreciation of art and nature and family history is what has saved those that have been preserved. There are few witnesses left to recall their construction and little documentation has survived. Had research been done at an earlier date, much more could be known.

Cities with greatest concentration of sites are Fort Worth, San Angelo and Lubbock. One was found in Houston and one in San Antonio, none were found in El Paso, none in Dallas. Many more examples were found than could be covered in one book; those included were chosen for their striking appearance, historical documentation or location in an under-represented region, such as Donna in South Texas and Alpine in West Texas.

The term "stone-tree house" was used by local Hopi and Navajo residents to describe the Painted Desert Inn in northern Arizona. It was constructed in the early 1920s using petrified wood from the immediate area, north of the Petrified Forest National Park. The builder, Herbert Lore, used the term in brochures advertising the business to travelers on the newly opened Route 66. For purposes of this book, the term has been broadened to include a "rockhound mix" of any colorful and unusual stones, minerals and other fossils.

About Scott Singleton

Houston geophysicist Scott Singleton has contributed the information about fossil wood and the geology of Texas introducing each region.

An earth scientist and researcher with 30 years of experience in the oil industry, he initiated a project in 2000 to add to the body of scientific knowledge about fossil woods in the Texas Gulf Coast Cretaceous and Tertiary.

Plant "megafossils" are important because they are more common than leaves or fructifications and can be used in place of those plant structures for paleoclimatical reconstructions. In particular, fossil wood assemblages can be used to delineate the early Eocene warming trend, the late Eocene cooling trend, and the sudden transition to the cooler Oligocene climate.

His work seeks (1) to identify the taxonomy and range of silica-replaced wood in the Tertiary and Cretaceous of the northwestern Gulf of Mexico, and (2) to assess the paleoclimate using correlations between paleo and modern plant species assemblages and analysis of known wood anatomical climate indicators.

The collection, preparation, analysis, and identification of fossil woods within the study area currently involves over 700 thin section slides with about 25-100 being added per year.

Sampling within the study area totals about 100 localities between the Mexican and Louisiana borders, from the Late Pennsylvanian of Central Texas through the Cretaceous and Tertiary of Central and Coastal Texas. He has continued to write and publish during the course of the study; his publications are listed in the Appendix, and other articles can be found at the websites of the Houston Gem and Mineral Society (hgms.org, scroll down to "Petrified Wood Articles") and the Society for Amateur Scientists (sas.org).

We appreciate his permitting us to reproduce excerpts (Part 2. Methods, Collection and Sampling Procedures and Part 3. Other Corroborative Lines of Research, see Appendix C) from one of his studies, the (so-far) three-part series, *Anatomy of Fossil Woods and Paleoclimate in the Texas Gulf Coast Tertiary and Cretaceous: An Ongoing Research Project.*

MAP: Geology of Texas

ABOUT THE REGIONS

This book divides Texas broadly into seven regions as shown on the map. Within each region, the individual sites are arranged generally north to south.

KEY

—	Major Rivers
NW	Northwestern Region
W	Western Region
NC	North Central Region
NE	Northeastern Region
SC	South Central Region
SE	Southeastern Region
S	Southern Region

Era	Period	Age	Formation/Group
CENOZOIC	Quaternary	2 m.y.	Alluvium (Qal)
			Quaternary undivided (Qu)
			Beaumont Formation (Qb)
			Lissie Formation (Ql)
			Blackwater Draw Formation (Qbd)
	Tertiary	Pliocene 5 m.y.	Willis Formation (Pow)
			Ogallala Formation (PoMo)
		Miocene 24 m.y.	Goliad Formation (Mog)
			Fleming and Oakville Formations (Mof)
		Oligocene 38 m.y.	Catahoula Formation (Oc)
			Oligocene and Eocene undivided (OE) (volcanic rocks and conglomerates in Trans-Pecos Texas)
		Eocene	Jackson Group (Whitsett, Manning, Wellborn, Caddell, Yazoo, and Moodys Branch Fms.) (Ej)
			Claiborne Group (Yegua Formation) (Ec2)
		58 m.y.	Claiborne Group (Cook Mountain, Sparta, Weches, Queen City, and Reklaw Fms.) (Ec1)
		Paleocene	Wilcox and Midway Groups (EPA)
MESOZOIC	Cretaceous	66 m.y.	Navarro and Taylor Groups (Ku2)
			Austin, Eagle Ford, Woodbine, and U. Washita Groups (Ku1)
			Fredericksburg and L. Washita Groups (Kl2)
		144 m.y.	Trinity Group (Kl1)
			Cretaceous undivided (Ku)
	Jurassic Triassic 245 m.y.		Jurassic Triassic undivided (JT)
PALEOZOIC			Ochoan Series (Po)
			Guadalupian Series (Whitehorse Quartermaster Formations) (Pg2)
			Guadalupian Series (Blai San Angelo Formations (
			Leonardian Series (Pl)
		286 m.y.	Wolfcampian Series (Pw)
			Permian undivided (Pu)
			Virgilian Series (IPv)
			Missourian Series (IPm)
		320 m.y.	Desmoinesian Series (IPd)
			Atokan and Morrowan Series (IPam)
		505 m.y.	Mississippian, Devonian, and Ordovician undivided (MDO)
		570 m.y.	Cambrian (-C)
			Paleozoic undivided (Pau)
Precambrian		1200 m.y. 2000 m.y.	Precambrian undivided (p-C)

Geology of Texas courtesy of Bureau of Economic Geology, The University of Texas at Austin

Stone-Tree Houses of Texas

Map: Distribution of Stone-Tree Houses

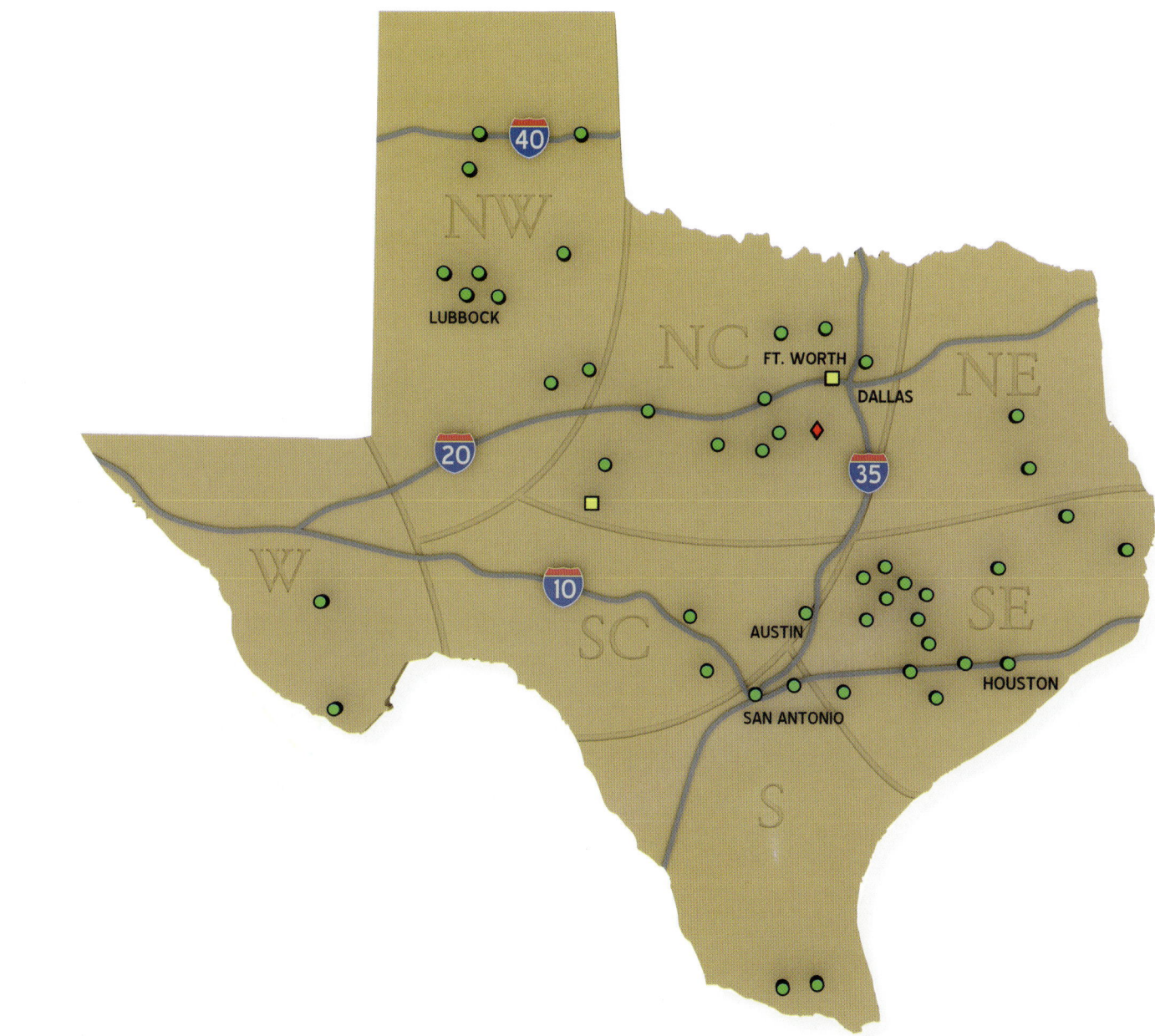

Northwestern/Caprock Region

About the Geology

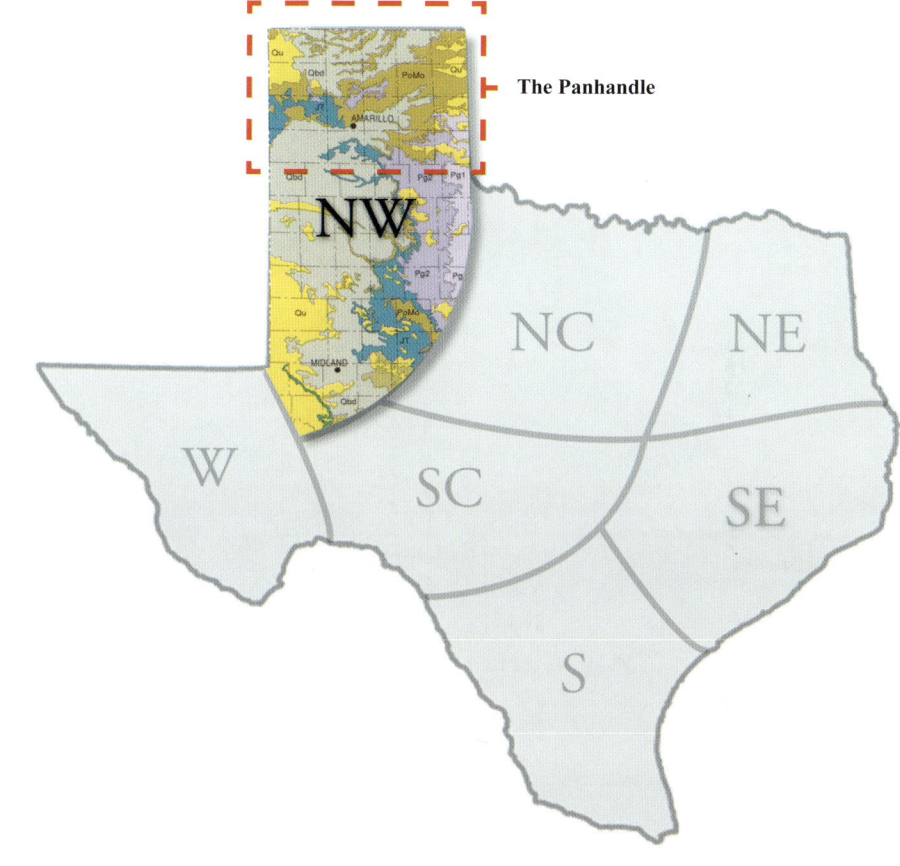

The Panhandle

The Ogallala Formation underlying northwest Texas is a thick series of gravel, sand, and clay layers shed between 10 and 4 million years ago from the newly rising Rocky Mountains to the west and northwest. (Spearing, 1991)

These layers originally formed a broad apron of coarse sediment from the foot of the ancestral Rocky Mountains through New Mexico, Colorado, and Wyoming to the middle of the Great Plains through Texas, Oklahoma, Kansas, Nebraska, and northward.

The remnant of this great apron in Texas and eastern New Mexico is called the Llano Estacado, or the Caprock. The Caprock is a layer of caliche (calcium carbonate) which is harder to erode than the material beneath it. This prolific unit is the basal conglomeratic member that rests unconformably on eroded Triassic Dokkum Formation sediments.

Based on the species mix of both animal and plant fossil assemblages, the environment was considered to be neotropical, similar to current day southern Mexico, Central America, and northern South America. Petrified woods in the Texas Panhandle are relatively common in fluvial (river) or lacustrine (lake) members of the Ogallala Formation, which is famous for its fossil flora and fauna. Most of the fossil woods are gymnosperms (conifers) but some angiosperms (hardwoods) are also present. Large trees eroded out of these sediments and were occasionally used in construction.

— *Scott Singleton*

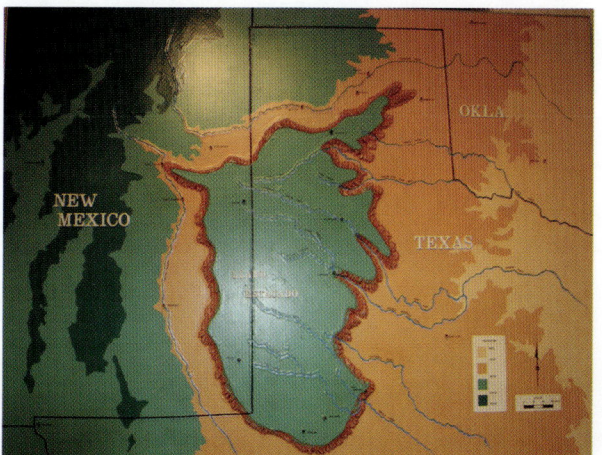

The 'Caprock' is actually a remnant of a great apron of coarse sediments which descended when the Rocky Mountains rose 10 to 4 million years ago. Also known as the Llano Estacado, this caliche plateau has endured as the surrounding plains eroded. A model (left) of the Caprock is located in the Llano Estacado Museum in Plainview and is the work of Director Rodney Watson.

Alanreed: Bruce Nursery

'The Show Place of the Panhandle'

According to family lore, the Bruce clan emigrated from Scotland to East Texas in the mid-1800s, moving further west in 1902 to homestead a farm at Clarendon in Donley County, where the "improvements" consisted of a half dugout and a water well. Paul Bruce married in 1918, became disenchanted with farming and the "two bits a bushel" paid for a crop of white corn and turned to selling fruit trees, traveling a 60-mile route while keeping an eye out for vacant land suitable for his tree farm and nursery business.

At the edge of the Caprock near Alanreed (Gray County) and the old stage line from Clarendon he found 80 acres – with another dugout, a windmill, and no road. For the first few years he and his growing family had to drive on the creek bed; the only way to get to the site chosen for the house was so steep that cars had to go up the slope in reverse. But the bottomland of McClellan Creek at an old Native American winter campground proved to be the perfect location for his long-dreamed-of orchard. Route 66 came to Alanreed in 1928. As son Robert Bruce tells it, one day while filling up his Model T at one of the new service stations, Robert's father noticed a piece of petrified wood and asked about it. The attendant told him he could have all he wanted from

Small pieces of fossil wood inlaid in 1929 spell out the Bruce name over the entrance to the original building, which served as a home and office for the next 30 years. Paul Bruce and his sons continued to collect the petrified wood stones locally to build other buildings on the property as the family and the business grew.

Always experimenting, Paul Bruce worked with Texas A&M to develop fruit trees, shade trees and other nursery stock that would withstand such Texas-style misfortunes as late freezes, perennial drought and voracious rabbits.

the pasture so the Bruce boys were put to work gathering and hauling the stones which were to be used to build the family's house.

They did the work in stages. By the fall of 1929, work had begun on the foundation and an 18-inch footer strong enough to carry the petrified wood walls. A flatcar of lumber for the framing was delivered to the railway depot in 1930, Mr. Bruce framed in the walls, the doors and the 26 windows and rocking began in 1931.

Initially, Mr. Bruce contracted with a McLean bricklayer, "Preacher Hunt," who began laying the rocks in neat, orderly rows. Objecting, Mr. Bruce said that he wanted the rock laid "as rough as it was found." When the bricklayer didn't think that he could do the work that way, Robert's father decided that he and his sons and various family members could do the job themselves. Robert says that they "fit the stones together like a jigsaw puzzle," with the rocks only shaped where necessary to complete an angle. The two sons spent most of the next decade rocking the buildings. The depression had "set in hard" that year and the construction provided steady work to many family members and friends during a time when work was scarce.

Paul Bruce remained in the nursery business throughout his working life, growing much of his own stock and pioneering many dry land crops and fruit tree varieties now commonplace in the region. He also continued to use petrified wood stones in the construction of additional structures on the property into 1960s.

His son Robert also built his own house on the grounds with the fossilized wood. Through the years, the community-minded family often opened the orchards to the public, hosting gatherings and festivals, and the Bruce Nursery became well known for its beautiful buildings and grounds.

All old photos courtesy of the Bruce family

Two of the Bruce boys, Robert and Truman, spent the better part of a decade working with their dad to rock the Bruce Nursery buildings.

The Bruce Nursery was a family business.

On a family outing, infant Robert Bruce was behind the wheel; he had to wait until he was 12 to get a driver's license.

Pioneering horticulturist Paul Bruce

A Bruce family Christmas card

A petrified yucca can be found in the hearth. Crystalline rock from Hot Springs, Ark., was inlaid in the enclosed front porch.

A painting of the Bruce Nursery office and home.

The McLean News touted the nursery and grounds as 'The Show Place of the Panhandle' with a front-page photo in 1938.

The Bruces hosted many gatherings through the years on the grounds of their nursery.

A rounded, two-story 'tower' connects to a corner of the building.

Stacked fossil logs create a stone tree on the chimney.

Paul M. and Ethel Bruce

The greenhouse at the Bruce Nursery no longer stands, but it was constructed originally with highly colored flint from the Alibates Flint Quarries (now a national monument). It was attached to the main house by a rock wall of petrified wood. It is theorized that many outbuildings and hardscape features surrounding stone-tree buildings resulted from the fact that so much material was required to successfully complete the 'jigsaw puzzle' of natural pieces in the main structure.

Paul Bruce wanted the stone in the walls of his nursery laid 'as rough as it was found.'

The Bruce Nursery, c.1950, and a Studebaker Land Cruiser

In later years, a carport was added to the original two-car garage.

Photos from the Bruce family's scrapbook show some changes in the house and landscaping over the years.

Whole sections of petrified wood logs decorate the chimney; carefully chosen large pieces were also used for the door lintels and window casings.

Northwestern Region

Amarillo: McCollum House

The McCollums spent 10 years collecting distinctive stones from all parts of the country to rock their house in Amarillo in 1939. Twenty tons of fossil wood were trucked in from New Mexico.

'Dream Home in Amarillo'

According to the April 1, 1946, issue of the Amarillo Daily News, Osburn R. McCollum, a paint contractor, and his wife Myrtle had spent some 10 years collecting the more than 100 tons of rocks they used for their house on Travis Street in Amarillo (Potter County). It was built in 1939.

"O.R." was working in Tucumcari, N.M., where he'd made a deal (that included a few cold beers) with a rancher who had petrified wood, which the couple especially prized. About 20 tons were collected from his property.

As Betty Gose's column described, the rocks included: "... mahogany and gray granite from Oklahoma, pink stone from Milsap, rock candy and colored rock from Flomot, shell rock from Houston, lava from near Dallas and New Mexico, petrified dinosaur flesh from the LS ranch at Tascosa, a large piece of clear green rock from Glass Mountain in Montana, petrified wood from Tucumcari, Bowie and the Petrified Forest, skull rocks with identical hollows from San Antonio, and even two stalactites from Carlsbad Caverns. The last item was taken from the caverns long before it became a government park.

"Delicately shaded pink stone on one side of the house has live cactus about two inches high growing straight out from the

MONDAY MORNING
Petrified Dinosaur Goes Into Dream Home in Amarillo

By BETTY GOSE

The whim of a temperamental Latin-American nearly lost O. R. McCollum a whole truckload of special rocks for the building of his new home. For several weeks McCollum, a paint contractor, had been bringing carloads of hand-picked stones from Tucumcari in his car back to Amarillo, but decided to hire a truck to haul the balance in one trip.

Arrangements were made and the hauler agreed to bring the load of rocks to McCollum one Saturday afternoon. The day wore on and the next—still no truck from Tucumcari. Monday, the paint contractor returned to Tucumcari, where he was working on the new courthouse and looked up his truck driver. It turned out that the man had gotten tired of driving when he reached Adrian and proceeded to unload the whole business at the nearest filling station.

It took McCollum a week to get a signed statement from the truck driver and prove to the garage owner that the rocks belonged to him.

* * *

The quest for unusual rock grew out of a 10-year-old desire to build a home entirely of colorful stone and petrified wood.

In that time Mr. and Mrs. McCollum managed to collect more than 100 tons of assorted rocks that went into the construction of a six-room house at 1510 Travis. It was built in 1939.

More than 20 tons of rock and petrified wood came from around Tucumcari while McCollum was working there. Every Saturday afternoon when the Amarillo construction crew came home for the week end they would load up their cars and pickups to capacity and bring the rocks over.

* * *

Petrified wood was the main thing McCollum was after. He learned that a rancher near Tucumcari had great quantities of the stone on his property, so McCollum contacted him, to discuss an arrangement to buy several loads of the stone and other special rocks. The owner insisted there was no such special rocks on his place and even took McCollum over parts of the ranch to prove his point.

But McCollum was not discouraged. On his second visit, he loaded up a five-gallon pail full of ice cold beer and went calling. After an hour of conversation and several bottles of brew, McCollum brought up the rock subject again. This time he drew a flicker of interest from the rancher and an admission that maybe he did have some after all.

The two men took another tour over the ranch via a different route and there McCollum found a wealth of petrified wood and unusual rocks. He struck up a satisfactory deal with the rancher and in that manner acquired most of the material he needed.

* * *

Random selections of stones in the house show that there are mahogany and gray granite from Oklahoma, pink stone from Milsap, rock candy and colored rock from Flomot, shell rock from Houston, lava from near Dallas and New Mexico, petrified dinosaur flesh from the LS ranch at Tascosa, a large piece of clear green rock from Glass Mountain in Montana, petrified wood from Tucumcari, Bowie and the Petrified Forest, skull rocks with identical hollows from San Antonio and even two stalagtites from Carlsbad Caverns. The last item was taken from the caverns long before it became a government park.

* * *

Delicately shaded pink stone on one side of the house has live cactus about two inches high growing straight out from the wall, while pieces of petrified wood are covered with moss. Prize rock collections include a small specimen called rose rock because it is always shaped in the form of a half blown rose. Another pink stone, dubbed Indian Money, is carved by nature with six symetrical sides about the size of a silver dollar.

Much care and precision were put into the placing of the rocks. No two similar stones or colors are cemented together. Tops of the windows and doors are set off by vertical cylindrical rocks all the same length. A note of elegance is added by the polished marble window ledges which were made of scraps from the Childress courthouse.

* * *

Most fascinating feature of the house is the petrified tree built into the chimney. McCollum found a whole tree near Tucumcari complete with branches. As much of this as possible was incorporated in the chimney with a carved red clay squirrel crouching on one of the top limbs. A large "M," fashioned of iron, fits on the front side of the chimney.

In the back yard a valuable piece of petrified wood about three feet long and two feet thick, is used for a bench. A worn hollow shows the effect of repeated use of a crude ax. The 400-pound stone came from Tucumcari.

Along the top of the rock fence are pieces of petrified wood which came from one tree. McCollum found the specimen in a heap which looked as if the tree had suddenly collapsed and splintered. Back of the house a frame four-room apartment is built on top of the stone garage.

* * *

Not all the beautiful pieces of rock are found on the outside walls. More delicate bits of stone, gyp and minerals were used in the fireplace. Pieces of copper and gold from a New Mexico gold mine reflect the light, as do the pyrites, worthless shiny metals. One block of red petrified wood in the fireplace can be found only in northern New Mexico. What almost turned into a diamond is the crystal from Arkansas which makes the more eye-arresting pieces in the fireplace. Long precision-made fingers of crystal were made into the snowflake-like patterns entirely by gasses.

Enough rocks have been left over to build an outdoor fireplace someday. Except for that, the house is complete, built just to individual ideas and needs. The McCollums have their dream home as a sharp contrast to the frantic searching of today's refugees from the housing shortage.

Symphony in Rock

In her column for the *Amarillo Daily News*, Betty Goss told her readers about the McCollums' house, describing the acquisition of much of the petrified wood, details of laying the stone and naming many of the special stones the McCollums brought back from their trips to use in its construction.

Archival material provided by the Amarillo Public Library and courtesy of the Amarillo Globe-News

wall, while pieces of petrified wood are covered with moss.

Prize rock collections included a small specimen called rose rock because it is always shaped in the form of a half blown rose, another pink stone dubbed Indian Money is carved by nature with six symetrical (sic) sides about the size of a silver dollar." She goes on to comment on the placement of the stones and the soldier courses over the windows:

"Much care and precision were put in the placing of the rocks. No two similar stones or colors are cemented together. Tops of the windows and doors are set off by vertical cylindrical rocks all the same length. A note of elegance is added by the polished marble window ledges which were made of scraps from the Childress courthouse."

Of particular note was the chimney. Apparently, O.R. had discovered a whole petrified tree on the rancher's land, "complete with branches," which he used on the chimney. The little carved squirrel hidden in its branches may be the "signature" of a stonemason from Moran named Bill Garrett (pg. 34).

The fireplace in the six room house was constructed with the same care using "delicate bits of stone, gyp and minerals ... pieces of copper and gold ... pyrite ... crystal," all of which would gleam in the light of the fire.

A 'tree' created with fossilized logs inlaid in chimneys is a recurring stylistic theme found on several stone-tree homes in the Caprock region (Shadden House, pg. 30 and the Moore House, pg. 52). O.R. McCollum found a complete stone tree near Tucumcari, N.M., which he reassembled and mortared into the chimney.

The stone squirrels found in the chimneys of the McCollum and Shadden homes (pg. 10 and page 30) may have been a signature of stonemason Bill Garrett.

Amarillo: Heath House

Pieces of petrified wood, fossils, conch shells and unique stones surrounding a heart-shaped arrangement of small seashells were used to create the fireplace in the Heath House.

The Story of My Life — By Thelma O'Neal Heath

I was born in Glen Rose, Texas, April 18, 1901 along with my twin brother, Thurman.

... we built a rock house at 2500 Polk, moved there in Feb. 1947, and lived there until Ross retired in Sept. 1961.

Thelma Heath left a hand-written record of her story.

'A rock house like no other'

According to their descendants, Elbert Ross (E.R.) and Thelma (O'Neal) Heath rocked two houses on Polk Street in Amarillo (Potter County).

E. R. and Thelma bought their first home in the 1700 block, their second a few blocks east; they also rocked their house in Rainbow when they retired. They were originally from around Glen Rose, so they were familiar with using petrified wood in construction.

A locomotive engineer for the Pacific and Santa Fe Railroad, E.R. always worked "extra board" on the trains instead of a regular schedule which would "interfere with his rock hunting."

Every year he and Thelma went on vacation in their old pickup, pulling a trailer. They gathered petrified wood and other native stone from around Amarillo – from Palo Duro Canyon, the Canadian River, Panhandle campgrounds, state parks, Alibates, Lake Meredith – later ranging further afield to Oklahoma, New Mexico, Colorado, even west to Oregon and California. They collected quartz in Arkansas, sandstone in Arizona and even "snuck a little stuff they weren't supposed to" out of the Redwood National Forest. The story goes that he personally visited 30 states to collect specimens and eventually acquired rock from all 48 states, including a special rock from Rhode Island, as well as others from Alaska and Mexico; that a lot of the white sand used in the mortar came from Alamagordo; and that people would arrive with knapsacks full of rocks from the Appalachian Trail, the New England states and other far away places. The stones were piled up on the corner lot.

In 1947, the City of Amarillo issued a building permit for a five-room "stone veneer" house and in 1948, the city directory lists the Heaths at their new address.

Mr. Heath wanted to build "a rock house like no other" and he didn't want anyone else to put it together. After the frame was sheathed, he enlisted the assistance of his brother, his sons, his fellow railroaders and – Thelma. Mr. Heath's grandson remembers that his grandmother did lay the stones – he helped her mix up mortar and lift rocks; he says she would take something like an old metal washtub, mix up some mortar and put rock around it.

All black and white images courtesy of descendants of the Heath family

The Heath House was completed in 1947.

The Heaths covered two houses in Amarillo with stone. Above, Thelma, who did some of the masonry herself, posed on the front porch of their first house before and after it was rocked.

Men of the Heath family also fished.

The first house still lacked plantings.

Ross Heath did much of the rock work on his second stone-tree home.

16 • *Stone-Tree Houses of Texas*

We built a house on the banks of the Brazos River in Rainbow, Texas. We went to Church at Cleburne. We entertained a lot and enjoyed our retirement.

Carrying on their tradition after retirement, Mr. and Mrs. Heath added rock to yet another house at Rainbow. Though not fully clad, the house is surrounded with stone wainscoting and features a stone and petrified wood chimney.

The Heaths' grandson remembers helping his grandmother lay stone.

Canyon: Buffalo Courts

The first athletic dorm in the state

Construction of the first athletic dormitory in the state began in 1934, for the West Texas State Teachers College, now West Texas A&M University, in Canyon (Randall County). Named as a tribute to the school's mascot, the Buffalo Courts complex was built by student athletes and Depression-era workers who transported tons of richly colored petrified wood and other native stones collected in the Canadian River breaks and nearby tributaries of the Red River, as well as a few from Carlsbad Caverns in New Mexico. Rocks were also sent from "virtually every state," according to local newspaper reports.

The finished structures included 22 dormitory rooms, a two-story recreation hall with fireplaces and an upstairs dance floor, staff offices, dressing rooms, a field house, a full-size swimming pool, croquet grounds, tennis courts and a 3,000-seat stadium with bleachers, all rocked in with fossil wood and surrounded by a rock wall. Construction, headed up by Gus Miller and one carpenter, continued until the early 1940s.

During the 1980s and '90s, the West Texas A&M University Alumni Association completed several renovations to the only building in the complex which had not been razed, the recreation hall; the restored building now serves as the WTAMU Alumni Center and in 2007 was designated a Recorded Texas Historic Landmark.

The following summary of the story of the Buffalo Courts was issued by the WTAMU Alumni Association.

A Brief History of the Buffalo Courts

In 1933, the concept of the Buffalo Courts Athletic Dormitory at West Texas State Teachers College (now West Texas A&M University) was suggested by Coach Al Baggett, head of the West Texas Athletic Department, and C.H. Jarrett, pharmacist, president of the Canyon Athletic Club, and Mayor of Canyon. Buffalo Courts would be the first strictly athletic dormitory in the state, designed to house 55 students.

The Canyon Athletic Club started the fund raising project: R.A. Terrill, editor of the Canyon News, began various activities to raise money; and the state legislature appropriated funds. Funds and grants for Buffalo Courts totaled $150,801.00, including a grant from the Works Progress Administration.

All together the W. P. A. funded more than $200,000 in campus improvements including Stafford Hall (still in use today); a home economics dormitory: El Pueblo—a structure designed for married students; an addition to Cousins Hall; and campus streets.

The Federal Emergency Relief Administration hired students from the college to help build Buffalo Courts, and construction began on August 22,

All black and white photos and clippings courtesy of WTAMU and the Panhandle Plains Historical Museum

Head of the West Texas Athletic Department, Coach Al Baggett, who spearheaded the construction of the first athletic dormitory in the state, confers with business manager Travis Shaw, who found a seat on a fossil wood log.

One of the finished Buffalo Courts buildings; note the stack of 'logs' of petrified wood awaiting placement.

1934, on the site of the home of the original college mascot, the buffalo. The rooms were arranged around a patio in a "U" shape, approximately 138 feet on each side.

In front of the patio rose the recreation hall, a large two-story building of petrified wood and native stone which was not completed until 1941 and is the only part of the structure still standing.

Buffalo Courts was the architectural wonder of the United States. Syndicated sportswriters carried stories of the West Texas Athletic Department and the athletic dormitory.

The lower floor of the recreation hall held a 38'x 42' reception room. At each end was large fireplace constructed of stone and faced with native Texas petrified wood. A massive staircase led to the second floor, where a large dance floor of hardwood was used for receptions and open houses, and two large fireplaces adorned each end of the room, faced with crystal and stone from Carlsbad Caverns.

In the mid nineteen eighties the University Alumni association was looking for a place to call home. Although Buffalo Courts was in major need of a face-lift, it was a "place" and the Alumni Association moved in.

After a renovation project which created an office for the director and replaced badly needed items such as carpet and ceiling tiles, the Association had a place of which they could be proud and which served their purposes perfectly. A permanent place on campus that Alumni remembered for its uniqueness and history.

In 1994 an additional renovation project took place to provide for a reception area for Alumni Association and University functions. Thanks to the generosity of the T Club, the

The 'grand staircase' leads to the dance floor upstairs in the building that now houses the WTAMU Alumni Association Center.

organization of former athletes (many of whom had lived in the Courts), the upstairs was upgraded to provide that area. That room remains today the T Club Reception Hall in honor of "the men who called Buffalo Courts home and those committed to the preservation of this historical structure."

On October 5, 2002 the WTAMU Alumni Association hosted a Grand Reopening for the Buffalo Courts Alumni Center. After undergoing the most extensive renovation project ever, Buffalo Courts is now home to the Milton "Buff" Morris Board Room, memorializing the founding Executive Secretary of the Alumni Association; a new suite of offices; and a full kitchen for hosting events.

Combined with elegant new furnishings and artwork by Kenneth Wyatt, the Buffalo Courts Alumni Center now provides a campus "home away from home" for alumni and friends of West Texas A&M University.

Two-story chimneys at either end of the Buffalo Courts Recreation Hall serve fireplaces in the only original building still standing.

Money
$10,000 BILL PASSED WORK ON CAMPUS

Swimming Pool is Given $2,500 In the Bill Passed

$7,500 FOR COURTS

Governor Yet To Act Upon Bill for the Money

An emergency appropriation for W. T. in the sum of $10,000 was passed by the legislature Tuesday and is now in the hands of the Governor. This money was voted for the purpose of completing Buffalo Courts, completing work on Burton Gymnasium, building the rock wall around the athletic field and completing the repair work in the swimming pool in the administration building.

In the bill $7,500 was allowed for the athletic field program, and $2,500 for the swimming pool.

The request for the money was taken to Austin a month ago by Travis Shaw, business manager of W. T. He took pictures of the work now under way at Buffalo Courts, and the need of repairing the swimming pool. The fact that relief work was being used, and would be available for several weeks to come was emphasized in asking this amount for materials on these projects. Senator Clint Small pushed the bill through the Senate last week, and Representative H. K. Stanfield sponsored the bill when it came before the House this week.

According to Coach Al Baggett the $7,500 for materials will be sufficient to guarantee the completion of most of the work now

Construction underway at the Buffalo Courts

The Recreation Hall

The Buffalo Stadium incorporated a design of the WTAMU buffalo mascot above one of the two entrances. Period images and clippings reflect the progress of the construction at Buffalo Courts.

Relief Work at Buffalo Courts Is Authorized

Fifty Men Put to Work Tuesday After Lay Off in Labor During the Month

Fifty men were put to work Tuesday on Buffalo Courts from the local relief office when appeal was made Monday by Coach Al Baggett to the district office at Amarillo for men to complete this work.

The men will work 40 hours this week, and indications are that 40 hours will be allowed them next week.

This is the first work that has been given men on the relief rolls since the middle of July.

The new district supervisor expressed great interest in the Buffalo Courts project and would do every thing possible to keep men at work until it is finished.

Coach Baggett has about 50 boys who must be housed in the Courts with the opening of W. T. Every possible means will be taken to rush the work so that these boys may be housed comfortably in the new quarters.

Baggett Wishes Trees For The Buffalo Courts

Coach Al Baggett is asking for 500 trees to be used in beautification of Buffalo Courts. About 150 trees have been given to the project.

Mr. Baggett has started a nursery north of the Courts to take care of the trees ready to be set be well cared until such a be permanentl

Work on th projects were after the shut account of th is hoped that be completed during the c days.

An emergen passed the s for funds to f ish all work o to repair the s administration has not been House.

Rapid Progress to Be Made in Building of Rock Walls

Under the direction of Gus Miller, six local rock layers and six from Amarillo are laying the rock walls of Buffalo Courts and the fence around Buffalo Stadium. The Amarillo men were started to work Monday under WPA.

It has been unofficially anounced that reductions in WPA will start on March 15th. With this in mind, the six men from Amarillo were started Monday in order to insure that all of the rock walls be completed before any reduction was started.

Mr. Miller completed all of the foundations for the rock walls last week and is superintending erection of the walls. He has had charge of all of the rock work so far completed on the campus.

Work Progressing on Buffalo Courts

During the time of a depression is usually found retrenchment and curtailment of expansion, but just the reverse has been true on the campus of West Texas State Teachers College.

Throughout the past year several projects have been inaugurated by the Physical Education Department under the leadership of Coach Al Baggett, which are transforming the campus from just an ordinary college campus into one of the most beautiful, extraordinary landscapes that has ever been seen in the Panhandle.

Primary in the program of construction is the erection of a large dormitory for the athletes of the college.

Natural rock, petrified wood, and sand and gravel, all of which come from the Panhandle itself are the building material of the Buffalo Courts, as the construction is called.

ENTRANCE TO BUFFALO STADIUM EAST OF BURTON GYMNASIUM.

Labor is furnished by the boys themselves working under the FERA with the aid of one carpenter and one rock mason. The courts are to be a low, rambling, ranch-like structure, typical of the Panhandle. They are to be built in a U formation with a large recreational hall in the center.

There will be eleven rooms on each side. The rooms will be in apartments with a toilet and showers between each two rooms.

One wing of the courts has been completed and has aroused much interest in the district. In the breaks of the Canadian River and the arroyos of the Palo Duro Canyon have been gathered the stone and petrified wood which have combined to give Buffalo Courts a very unique appearance. "A new type of architecture, typical of the Panhandle," is the description given the completed wing by most of the visitors.

RECREATION HALL AND PART OF BUFFALO COURTS.

Rich color is given the buildings from the stone—rose and brown and gray which mingles with the gray tans and tawny greens that are to be found everywhere in the West Texas landscape.

On the inside of the rooms, everything is in harmony with the unique exterior. The inside finish is of rough plaster, with the woodwork given a burned stain effect by going over it with a blow torch. Hinges, door latches, and other hardware fixtures have been pounded, giving them an antique appearance.

The furniture consists of double deck bunks, table, chairs and book stands in each room, and all are sturdy enough to withstand rough usage. The 22 rooms when completed, will accommodate 92 boys.

On one side of the Courts will be a desert garden with shrubs and cacti typical of the Southwest, and on the other side will be a luxurious sunken garden in contrast to the desert flora.

With the completion of the one unit of the Buffalo Courts, an episode of building of the farmers

SHOWING FURNITURE OF ROOM IN BUFFALO COURTS.

Local paper *The Canyon News* and others tracked the process of securing federal, state and local funding, evidencing the support and interest of the community for the project.

Native stone and petrified wood piled high at the Buffalo Courts construction site

WPA rockmasons and students did much of the construction on the buildings.

To Open Buffalo Courts Monday

Monday Evening From 7:00 to 8:00 For Inspection

SHORT PROGRAM

Citizens Invited To See Work Which Is Under Way

Formal opening of the Buffalo Courts for an inspection of the public will be held next Monday evening from 7:00 to 8:00 o'clock.

An hour's inspection with a short program is being sponsored by the Canyon Athletic Club, the Chamber of Commerce and the Physical Education department of W. T.

All citizens of Canyon are asked to drive down to the Courts Tuesday evening and see what is being done in the way of construction and furnishing the rooms for the athletes of W. T. One or more of the units will be opened for public inspection so that the furniture may be seen by the visitors.

The two soft ball games scheduled for Monday evening will be played under the lights of Buffalo field at 8:00 o'clock instead of being played at 7:00 o'clock on the regular field.

Students of W. T. will join in greeting the citizens of Canyon and the visitors who will come to make an inspection of the new construction which is underway.

Coach Al Baggett is very anxious to meet all citizens of Randall county upon this occasion.

Lemonade will be served to the visitors.

The formal opening of the Buffalo Courts merited a big headline in *The Canyon News*.

The completed complex included the large recreation hall with dormitories on either side as well as a 3,000-seat stadium, swimming pool, field house and other structures.

Buffalo Courts also served as barracks and a parade ground during World War II.

Although all the buildings were not completed until 1941, the cornerstone inscription dates the beginning of construction to 1935.

The West Texas A&M University Alumni Association renovated the original Buffalo Courts Recreation Hall.

Northwestern Region 23

The entrance to the WTAMU Alumni Association Center is flanked by large colorful fossil wood logs. The building today is surrounded by the West Texas A&M University campus.

BUFFALO COURTS

A UNIQUE COMMUNITY VENTURE AT WEST TEXAS STATE TEACHERS COLLEGE DURING THE GREAT DEPRESSION PRODUCED AN ARCHITECTURAL LANDMARK. THE PROJECT BEGAN IN 1933 AND USED STUDENT LABOR, COMMUNITY DONATIONS, AND STATE AND FEDERAL FUNDING. LIMESTONE, PETRIFIED WOOD AND OTHER ROCK WAS QUARRIED IN TEXAS AND NEW MEXICO. THE COMPLEX INCLUDED A FIELDHOUSE, ATHLETIC DORMITORIES, AN OUTDOOR SWIMMING POOL, STONE WALLS AND STADIUM BLEACHERS. MUCH OF THE FACILITY WAS LATER RAZED; ONLY THE TWO-STORY RECREATION HALL COMPLETED IN 1941 REMAINS STANDING. THE FACILITY HAS A PETRIFIED WOOD EXTERIOR, LARGE STONE FIREPLACES AND STAIRCASE, AND A SECOND-STORY HARDWOOD DANCE FLOOR. IN THE 1980s, THE ALUMNI ASSOCIATION MOVED ITS HEADQUARTERS HERE.

RECORDED TEXAS HISTORIC LANDMARK - 2007
MARKER IS PROPERTY OF THE STATE OF TEXAS

The south fireplace and its upstairs (top) and downstairs hearth (below)

The north fireplace and its upstairs (top) and downstairs hearth (below)

The interior of the refurbished Recreation Hall features large petrified wood and stone fireplaces on both ends of the building which extend through both floors. The floors are connected by a fossil wood stairwell.

Northwestern Region

Matador: Bob's Cook Shack

'West Texas' finest cafe ...'

Bob's Cook Shack was part of the complex known as Bob's Oil Well at Matador (Motley County), opened by Luther Bedford "Bob" Robertson in 1932. Located midway between Sweetwater and Pampa where U.S. 70 intersects Texas 70, the towering oil derrick covered with lights constructed over the station could be seen for miles. "Bob" arranged with truckers to promote his place with signs posted on distant highways across the states. A sailor on a boat to Hawaii during the war reportedly passed an island in the Pacific with a sign advertising how many miles it was to Bob's Oil Well.

By the mid-'30s, Robertson had added a garage, a grocery, and a café built with red petrified wood and native stone, possibly collected near "Mrs. Campbell's Petrified Hill," as it was labeled on the old county maps. (She was one of the two women in the area in the late 1800s and postmistress of Matador Ranch.)

Although the business closed after his death, efforts to maintain and restore the buildings continue on the part of the Motley County Historical Commission, Motley Chamber of Commerce, City of Matador and Market Matador, as well as local rancher Marisue Potts and Robertson's granddaughter Princess Scaggs.

Bob's Oil Well was placed in 2004 on Preservation Texas' Most Endangered Places and in 2005 received a Texas Historical Commission Recorded Texas Historic Landmark plaque.

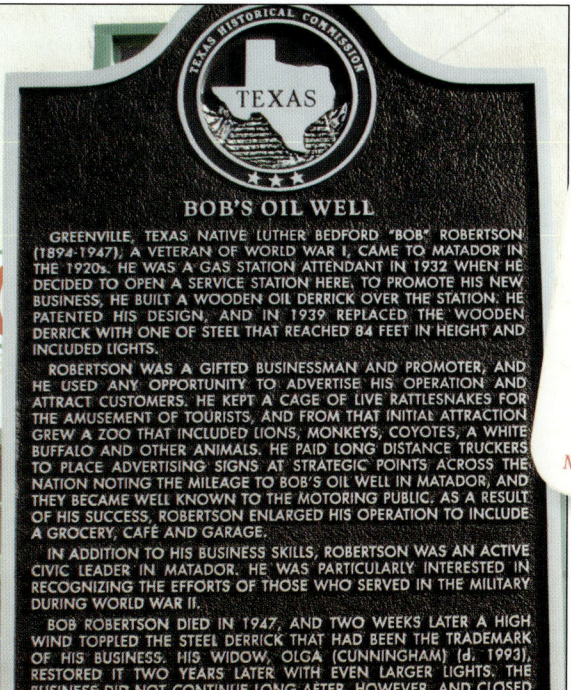

A Conoco promotional card for Bob's Oil Well and other memorabilia have been collected by the Motley Museum.

The design of the entrance to Bob's Cook Shack offered protection from wind in the winter months and also served as a 'wind scoop' to catch breezes in the summer.

Northwestern Region

The staff at Bob's in 1946 included waitresses Zelma Watson Crump and Isabell Muse, cook Ethel Timmons Pope, an unknown busboy and the dishwasher Mr. Donelson.

Two pages of the menu from 'Bob's Cook Shack'; a steak with fries and a drink was a dollar.

MATADOR, MOTLEY COUNTY, TEXAS, THURSDAY, 9-26-1946

West's Finest Cafe Is Opened In Matador

"Bob's Cook Shack" Contrast to Name

Fronting pavement that was once a wagon road over which Matador chuck-wagons have passed for three score and ten years, West Texas' finest cafe opened its doors to the public yesterday morning. It is fitting that here in Matador, in the shadows of the foothills of the Plains, should be located one of the most modern and elaborate restaurants between Albuquerque and Wichita Falls. Perhaps no one but L. B. (Bob) Robertson would have the vision and courage to invest the labor and money that has gone into the new "Bob's Cook Shack", which served its first customers yesterday morning.

Opening the new cafe closed the doors of the old "Bob's Cook Shack" where it is estimated more than a half million customers have been served on its 14 stools since first opening in 1933. The old cafe building will be converted into an automobile tire salesroom and repair department in connection with Bob's Oil Well service station. The new building is located about 40 feet south.

Bob Robertson has been buying a collection of petrified wood and colored stone for the past 15 years to build something. The material has gone into the 62 x 27-foot rock-veneer building. An estimated 20 tons of petrified wood alone was used in construction, in addition to the native rock and "imported rock." The beautiful dining room is 46 x 25 feet and the stainless steel-lined kitchen is 14 x 25 feet.

Bob Robertson took his time. The building was started March 1st. Materials were "impossible" to secure. "Old Bob" found them and built them into his cafe. No detail was overlooked. His plans were changed frequently but only to include more beauty or more customers or more modern equipment.

Outside, the colorful building has the appearance of a castle because of the three round storm door entrances. Two entrances are to the dining room; one west and one north, and one north entrance is to the elaborate kitchen, which cannot be entered from the dining room, but must be entered through the kitchen's storm door entrance on the outside. Food may be passed from the kitchen to the dining room anywhere along

The petrified wood buildings, a grocery, café and garage, adjoining the gas station were among the attractions for tourists and truckers on North Texas highways in the 1930s and '40s. Once a widely known pit stop, efforts to save Bob's Oil Well have been successful.

Bob Robertson Takes Own Life In Hotel Here
Colorful Career Ends In Tragedy

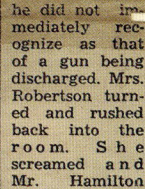

Final Rites Are Held Wednesday
1-16-1947

Bob Robertson is dead. A gun in his own hand wrote the final chapter in the history of Matador's most colorful character. Spirit of the amiable, 56-year-old, red-faced Irishman who rose from a filling station operator to one of this West Texas town's leading business men, is

LIGHTS were out on the tall tower of Bob's Oil Well Monday night and the Matador landmark service station was closed for the first time since it was opened about 14 years ago. The station and Bob's Cook Shack cafe have been closed since the tragedy and no announcement of arrangements had been made to a late hour yesterday.

released from mortal duty.

An inquest held shortly after his body was found in his Motley hotel room about 5:45 p.m. Monday afternoon, attributed his death to self-inflicted gunshot wound. He had been shot through the temple. A German Luger revolver was found near him. One shot had been fired from the weapon.

Former district attorney John Hamilton, Mr. Robertson's attorney in recent divorce proceedings, had been in the room with Mr. and Mrs. Robertson a few moments before the tragedy, discussing property settlement. As he started to leave the time he reached the lobby door, Mr. Hamilton declared he heard a sound which he did not immediately recognize as that of a gun being discharged. Mrs. Robertson turned and rushed back into the room. She screamed and Mr. Hamilton hurried up the stairs where he found the body prone on the floor. He rushed to the lobby and called sheriff John Stotts and Dr. J. S. Stanley. Mr. Robertson was pronounced dead upon arrival of the physician.

The inquest was conducted by County Judge Wm R. Cammack in the absence of Justice of the Peace Henry Pipkin.

Bob Robertson was perhaps better known than any individual in Motley County. He believed in Matador and the genius of hard work. He built an institution out of vision, magnetic personality and his ponderous industry. He had been a resident of Matador for 24 years.

Starting when other businesses were folding at the darkest hour of the depression in 1932, Bob Robertson took $100, a meager credit and his dream to open Bob's Oil Well filling station at the intersection of highways 70 and 18. Later he opened Bob's Cook Shack cafe adjoining the station. Following these two enterprises he opened Bob's Foodway grocery in what is now the district court room. About this time he constructed a new building and opened Bob's garage immediately east of the filling station. He later sold the grocery store and closed the garage, using the building as storage and for the repair of his fleet of Conoco trucks plying the highways in wholesale and retail distribution.

Immediately after its opening Bob's Oil Well service station became a Matador landmark. Constructed to represent an oil field derrick, the tower could be seen from many miles in any direction. By night it was brilliantly lighted. Bob's Oil Well road signs extended as far as three hundred miles in four directions from Matador. Travelers from over the entire nation stopped to visit his free zoo which at one time contained lions, buffalo, coyotes, monkeys and other animals. The cage of native rattlesnakes was a source of constant interest.

Newspaper clippings detail the death of Bob's Oil Well founder, Bob Robertson.

ABERNATHY: SHADDEN HOUSE

Stonemason brothers Bill and Tom Garrett built this rock house for Otey and Frona Mae (Land) Shadden in 1938-39. The filled-joint rock and fossil wood exterior incorporates stylistic motifs characterstic of the Garretts' stonemasonry.

Otey Shadden Jr. believes that his family came to be friends with the Garretts when his parents' house north of Abernathy (Hale County) burned down in 1938. One of the Garrett girls worked at the Shaddens' dairy farm, and the families vacationed in the mountains of Colorado, where they hunted rocks together.

The "tree" motif in the Shaddens' chimney resembles the tree in the McCollum house chimney (pgs. 12-13), complete with squirrel. The fireplaces in both houses are also similar. On the interior, as in the McCollum house, both fireplace hearths feature similar radial patterns with some very fine stone and fossil wood specimens in the interior hearth.

All old photos courtesy of the Shadden family

An oil painting of the house by daughter-in-law Sally Stanton Shadden hangs in their living room.

A Shadden family photo shows the home shortly after its completion in 1939.

Otey Shadden and his twin sister play on the porch; the home and the children were one year old.

Northwestern Region

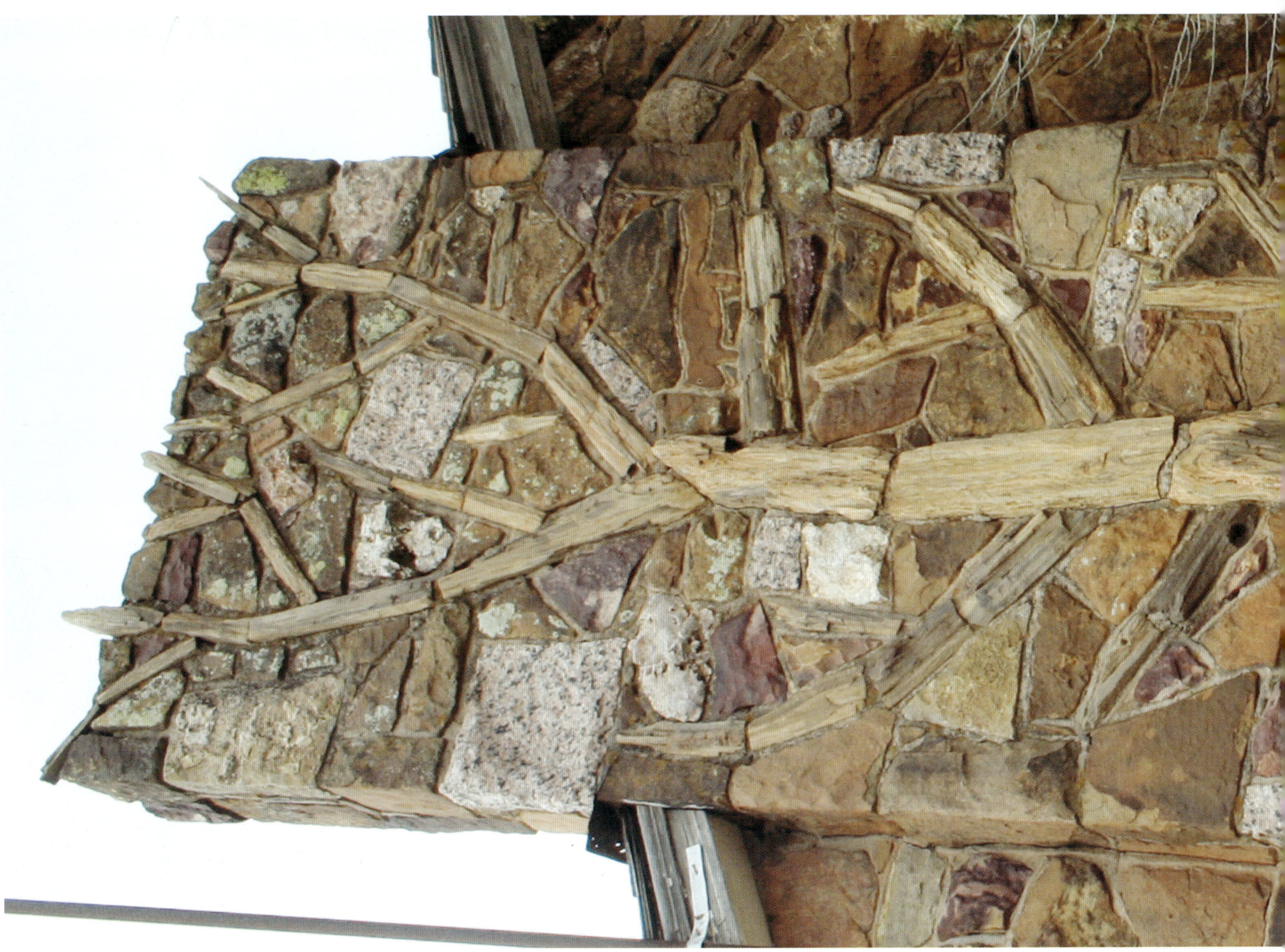

Squirrels sit in the branches of the petrified wood trees in both the Shaddon chimney and the McCollum chimney (pg. 12) and may be the 'signature' of stonemason Bill Garrett (pg. 34)

The Shadden hearth bears a striking resemblance to those in the McCollum (pg. 10) and Moore (pg. 52) houses, all three surely the work of Bill Garrett.

Northwestern Region 33

BILL GARRETT CAPROCK STONEMASON

Stonemason Bill Garrett (1903-1973) often working with his brother Tom, built various buildings in towns all over the Caprock.

Bill was known for the special touches in his work, such as squirrels in the branches of a stone tree. His mom said if he was in love, he would put a heart or a flower on the front of the house.

He was good friends with the Shaddens (pg.31) and Andersons of Abernathy and built the C.O. Anderson house there. Many of the walls and store fronts along Main Street in Abernathy are his work. He and C.O. Anderson spent a lot of time hunting rocks on the Caprock

Garrett lived for a time in Lubbock, and built his own rock house there which was later removed to make way for a school. Later he and the Shaddens purchased a lodge and cabins on a lake north of Durango, Colo. Bill rocked the cabins and a large fireplace in the lodge and for the rest of his life, spent his summers in Colorado.

A recent repair project of a wall around a cemetery at Moran uncovered more of Bill Garrett's work when workers discovered a whiskey bottle left inside the wall, the bottle contained a note revealing that Bill and his brother Tom along with Kenneth Fite built the wall in 1933 as part of a WPA project.

Tom Garrett made the front page of a special section of *The Albany News*. (See Appendix G, pg. 268)

John Garrett, Bill and Tom's father, was also a mason.

From left to right, Carl 'Skinny' Edgar, Bill and Dorothy Garrett and Bill's brother Tom Garrett. The three men worked as masons.

All old photos and clippings courtesy of the Garrett brothers' descendants

Masons hired to do some repair work at the Moran Cemetery discovered inside one of the walls an old whiskey bottle that contained a note, dated August 4, 1933, documenting the construction as part of a Works Progress Administration program and listing Kenneth Fite, Bill Garrett and Tom Garrett as the masons.

An old but undated photo from the Garrett family album captured a masonry crew on the job.

Bill Garrett built the Shadden fireplace, above at left, which shares stylistic similarities with the fireplaces in the McCollum House, at center, and the Moore House, at right. These fireplaces were built to use gas; the Moore's still retains the original insert.

An unusually steep gable tops the front door of the C.O. Anderson home in Abernathy. Completed in 1938, the detailed stonework is credited to Bill Garrett. A large number of smaller pieces of sandstone were used but granite and petrified wood are seen throughout. Cut sandstone soldier courses stand as lintels and multi-colored brick accents the window sills. C. O. and his brother R.H. Anderson were the contractors and carpenters for both their houses.

Northwestern Region

Abernathy: Anderson House

The R.H. Anderson House in Abernathy was built in 1938-39 using petrified wood and a wide assortment of other rocks.

The stonework on this home is attributed to "Dutch" (which in those years could have meant German) immigrants, who incorporated a sunflower motif as well as two decorative pinwheels into the design of the chimney; a second chimney features a branching fossil wood stone tree.

A repeated 'sunrise' or 'pinwheel' motif fills the gable ends of the Anderson house.

Hardscaping at the Anderson home includes several low walls richly decorated with colorful and unusual stones, glass, and fossil wood.

ANTON : BRAZIL HOUSE

The Brazil House near Anton has a mixed exterior composed primarily of sandstone with petrified wood. Because of the fine rockwork, the variety of specimen stone and the cut sandstone floral motifs at the gables, as well as the trademark sunflower and pinwheel designs on the chimney, it is believed that the house is the work of the same itinerant 'Dutch' immigrants who built the Anderson home on the previous pages.

Black and white photo courtesy of the Brazil family

Northwestern Region

Idalou: Knoles House

George Knoles struck it rich in 1918, when an oil gusher blew in next to his 80 acres in Desdemona. He sold out to an oil company for $75,000 (the equivalent of about $1.5 million today) and subsequently purchased a two-story ranch house on 748 acres in Lubbock County near Idalou. Sending his family ahead in their old Buick, he followed on the train, riding in the boxcar with the family's belongings, wagon and livestock – and all the cash in a suitcase.

For the next decade, the family worked the land and improved the property. A large pond fed by the overflow from a three-inch windmill, several big barns and other outbuildings were all added and the area around the existing house landscaped. George Knoles pursued several business interests over the years and the family owned and operated the local drugstore in the '20s. Their eldest son William (Bill), an avid rock collector, amassed a huge collection of stones, petrified wood and fossils on the property.

The Knoles divorced in 1927; in 1939, Martha Knoles decided to build a new house. The original farmhouse was dismantled and the wood used to frame the new building, which was constructed with a full two-room basement as well as a fireplace and arched entry ways. A local stonemason (possibly named Thornton), with the help of the "Snead Boys," Lester and Paul, rocked the walls with sandstone, limestone, granite, and fossil woods from Bill Knoles' collection. The chimney design included the tree motif popular in the Panhandle at the time – fossil wood logs arranged to imitate tree branches – and a large, uncut geode centered on the hearth inside. The petrified wood used is said to have been collected in New Mexico.

Martha and George remarried in 1953; he died in 1958 and she lived with her daughter Elizabeth in the home until her death at the age of 110.

The Knoles House was demolished in 2010.

Black and white photos courtesy of the Knoles family.

The original ranch house on the property was dismantled to provide wood for the new rock house. The later stone home (at left) was completed in 1939 and appears in this old family photo (double exposed).

Local stonemason Mr. Thornton is flanked by the tall 'Snead Boys' who helped rock Martha Knoles' new house.

Martha Knoles and her daughter Elizabeth were photographed with their stone-tree chimney as background.

Water from the windmill traveled through a 3-inch diameter pipe to feed the large pond behind the home.

The pond was big enough to float a boat.

The Knoles House, shown as it appeared in 2009, had been razed by 2010.

Lubbock: Fisher/Hufstedler House

In 1938, according to the Lubbock Historic Site Survey of 1985, R. J. (Robert Jackson) and Lillie M. Fisher contracted with Joe Telford, a well-known Lubbock (Lubbock County) contractor, to build a "six-room rock veneer" house.

That document describes an "unaltered … one-story stone residence w/ gabled roof and asphalt shingles on roof. Stone chimney rises through front façade. Arched entrance is located under asymmetrical gable. Large multi-light windows … small window next to doorway" and notes that it is "One of the residences built as Lubbock emerged from the Depression-induced building slump of the early 1930s."

The Lubbock city directory of 1938 listed Mr. Fisher's occupation as "sand and gravel."

Ernst Kiebler (E.K.) and Estelle Hufstedler bought the house in 1941 and moved in with their four children, who grew up there. In 1945, they remodeled the house, eliminating a side porch and extending the living room; the window was relocated and a basement dug about the length of the house and about half the length at the back. The attic was allocated to the three girls.

The asymmetrical roofline, pocket window and arched entry alcove lend a 'storybook cottage' feel to the Hufstedler home.

The Hufstedler family, E.K. Jr., Estelle, Don and his sisters Patsy, Sue and Linda, pose in the snow on the porch of their petrified wood house. Don Hufstedler believes that this photo is from the first Christmas they spent in the house in 1941.

The Fisher/Hufstedler House has been well-maintained since the 1940s.

Family photos courtesy of Don Hufstedler

The wide-shouldered chimney incorporates a sunflower motif very similar to those seen in the Anderson (pg. 36) and Brazil (pg. 40) homes.

Lubbock : Brunson House

'What a wonderful placed to be raised in'

Built by cattleman Stanton Brunson for his daughter in 1941 on land near Lubbock (Lubbock County) that he had acquired in the mid-30s, the large home was a showplace in its day.

The home features a low stone wall, red tile roof and full basement. The exterior is clad with a mix of sandstone, limestone and fossil wood punctuated by a distinctive black igneous (volcanic) rock. All of the specimens were collected from the same two-acre area on the L7 section south of Crosbyton.

Stanton Brunson's father, William, was a pioneering cattleman who operated a 60-section ranch in West Texas as early as the 1880s. The family eventually owned many large ranches and cattle operations in Texas, New Mexico and Mexico.

A typical gable end design mixed fossil woods, limestone, sandstone with the distinctive igneous rocks used throughout the façade.

All family photos courtesy of the Brunson family

Large pieces of petrified wood accent the surrounding perimeter wall.

Old snapshots of the Brunson House from the family scrapbook

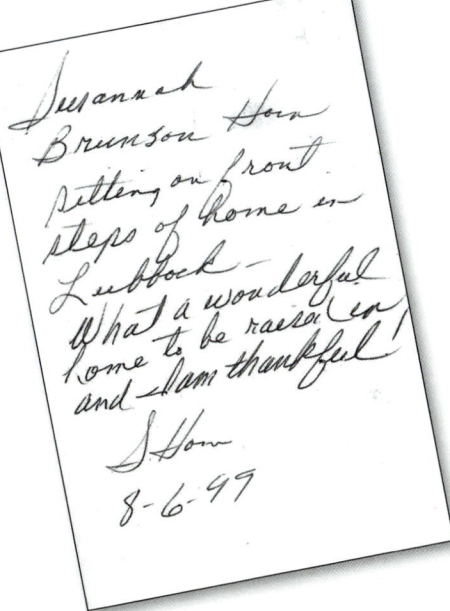

A note on the back of the photo at the left identifies the girl sitting on the porch steps as Stanton Brunson's daughter, Susannah.

A low stone wall surrounds the several buildings on the property.

Northwestern Region 51

Acuff : Moore House

The Moore House was completed in 1933. The rock work is a rich mosaic of smaller size stones interspersed with bits of fossil wood. Details include a buffalo skull set into the masonry and a petrified wood "tree" motif incorporated into the chimney similar to those seen in the McCollum (pg. 10) and Shadden (pg. 30) homes. The fireplace in this house shares characteristics of Bill Garrett's work.

Northwestern Region

The Moores used a flatbed trailer to haul stone from the San Saba area back to Acuff. The 1933 house was included in many of the family's photos.

Black and white photos courtesy of the Moore family.

Northwestern Region

ROTAN: VITTITOW HOUSE

Lonnie Clinton Vittitow, a barber by trade, and his wife Era traveled with a two-wheel trailer for more than a decade to collect the stones that they used on their house in Rotan (Fisher County) completed in the early 1950s. Mr. Vittitow checked out other masons' work for about a year before hiring "Mr. Neaves of Roby" to lay the rock.

Situated on a low rise at an intersection, the Vittitows terraced the slope with two low fossil wood walls.

Mr. Vittitow kept detailed records and dictated the story of collecting the rocks and building the house to his daughter, who typed it up and sent it to family members in 1964. It's reproduced below.

This is the history of the house at the Corner of Snyder and Genevieve streets in Rotan, Texas.
The house was purchased by L.C. Vittitow from W.C. White in 1945. After about two years, three rooms and a basement were added to the original construction. The work was done by a contractor, Richard Fleming.

An amethyst crystal in the arch above the front porch is the most expensive stone on the house; it was purchased from a 'medicine man.'

Northwestern Region 57

Some three years later we rocked the house from a collection of rocks which was begun twelve to fourteen years previously.

The history of collecting was a story in itself. Era and I had a 1933 Chevrolet and a two wheel trailer. On holidays and weekends we journeyed to nearby areas to get rocks. My first load came from Camp Springs. On a trip to Camp Springs we were perking down the road when a wheel rolled past the car. About that time the tongue broke out of the trailer and struck the ground and dumped the entire load of rock. These were limestone rocks. Later we got some granite in all colors from Dr. Young's ranch seven miles south of Roscoe, Texas. Era and I used a twelve pound sledge hammer to beat up the big boulders.

We got three loads of rock from Luders, Texas. These were yellow iron rock. About this time World War II occurred and about four years were lost as far as our collection was concerned, due to the fact of a gasoline and tire shortage.

The "Yellow Turkey Track" rocks came from Ellindale, Texas a small town east of Abilene. I lost my shirt on this trip! (It was eaten by the goats.)

Our next trip took us to Borden County where we got about 3,000 pounds of petrified wood, with the help of Bolivar Browning.

Near Sweetwater we collected some surface rock. On one trip we were on the way home when we realized that we had left our rock tools at the site. I unhitched the trailer, left Era and Charles with it and I returned for the tools, much to Era's dismay, but it has been something to laugh about over the years.

A hunting trip took us near Fort Worth, where we found some lovely sandstone, which we purchased and returned later with the trailer to pick up. Twenty five thousand, five hundred pounds of petrified wood came from Clyde, Texas. The man said that he had worked 6 years to get this out of his field with a one row tractor and slide. Dick Clements took his truck and went to Lamesa for Rainbow Rock. We got three squares of it.

Era and I went to Arkansas and Missouri to collect crystals. Most of these were put in the fireplace. During the time I was collecting rocks many relatives and friends contributed to the collection. As a result of these gifts I have rocks in the house from forty-three states and six foreign countries.

An ammonite fossil, a cast of the interior of a now extinct cephalopod, is embedded in this section of the wall.

A mosaic comprised of bits of fossil wood, colored stones and pebbles

One limestone rock came from Old Mexico. This rock came off a fence, which was said to be over two hundred years old. It is located on the north east corner of the home.

Truman got two magma rocks off Oahu Island, Hawaii in 1947. He brought them to the states on the Navy ship U.S.S. McDougal. One of these is near the front door and one is near the back door.

I bought a large crystal rock from Dr. Tate, a colorful medicine man, who brought his show annually to Rotan during the 30's and 40's. This rock is located on the arch at the front of the house. This is the most expensive rock in the house

One morning when I went to work there in the front of the barber shop door was a huge limestone rock, weighing about 150 pounds. A note was stuck on it, which said, "ask and ye shall receive!" Needless to say I had to roll the stone away before starting the days business.

One piece of petrified wood came from the farm adjoining the Petrified Forest in Arizona. It is Red. Mr. Foy brought a round rock from Ohio; it was placed on the north side of the house. In addition to crystals in the fireplace, there are rocks from the mountains of California gotten by Maggie Easterland in a burlap bag in country too rough to take a jeep. The coral came from Bikini Atoll at the atomic bomb test site.

The shell resembling a jackrabbit came from the Gulf of Mexico. Two small pieces in the fireplace came from Carlsbad Caverns. (Brought by friend, which shall remain anonymous since they did violate some rules to get it for us.)

We finally wore out the 1933 Chevy and got a 1939 Chevy and wore that one out too. We have three rocks that came from around Brownwood, Texas that have all kinds of things in them. Some look like elephant tusks and some look like teeth.

One rock I got from a man in San Angelo, Texas has petrified weeds in it. The weeds fell down and you can see the blooms on them. The individual rocks cost $35 to 15$ each. The rest of them cost $1.50 a square to $20 a square. Era and I can tell how much each rock in the house cost and where it came from.

The shells in the fireplace, which have the lights in them, came from Florida. The shell near the top was given to Era in 1903. The Abalone shell came from the west coast, brought by Truman and Claudine Vittitow. The blue fluoride crystal came from a mine in

Skilled masonry and joint work is seen throughout the Vittitow construction.

Illinois. And was brought up by a miner from a depth of 800 ft. Two small "bird eggs" rocks were brought from England by Carl Underhill. He also brought a piece of green urn from a bombed church in England and James Day brought a rock from South Africa. The six point crystal was sent by a friend from Hot Springs, Arkansas. The glass came from an abandoned glass factory in Santa Ana, Texas.

We got some rose rock from a gypsum site near Rotan. We had to climb a cow trail to get out of the canyon where we found it. The sides of the canyon were so steep that Era and Charles had to get behind me and push me up the sides of the canyon while I carried the rock. Once a ledge I was on caved off and I was buried almost to my waist in dirt.

Mr. Neaves of Roby laid the rock with the help of his son-in-law. It took two men forty-three days to lay the rock under the direction of Era Vittitow. During her supervision Era lacerated her hand and had 17 stitches to close the gap. She continued undaunted to the end of the 43 days. By this time L.C. had his fill of hamburgers and was eager for Era to return to her job in the kitchen.

There is a petrified wood a natural squirrel hole on the southwest corner of the house. One piece of petrified wood on the east side weighs 1000 pounds and it took 5 men to lay it. The foundation had 1400 feet of 3/8th inch steel cut on corners and tied in and 100 sacks of cement. It was run two years before the rocks were laid, it ranges from two to four feet In the ground and is eighteen inches wide. There are eighteen squares in the fence and eighteen in the house. The rock work has over 300 sacks of cement. The fence also has a foundation about eight inches wide and twelve inches deep. There are 504 inches of foundation and rock. There are two ledges; each is three feet, four inches high.

There is approximately 1900 feet of floor space in the house seven rooms and a basement. The basement is 12 x 14 feet. Since the house was rocked in 1950 at least one hundred people have come to look at it. The wall to the garage was started on November 2, 1963 and completes July 4, 1964. It is eighteen feet long and eleven feet high. I often worked on it in 100° temperatures.

Needless to say if we had it to do over, there are some changes we would make to the arrangement, but probably none in the appearance of the rocks outside. It is our lifelong dream come true and as we look back over the fourteen years of collecting and building we realize that our "hobby" provided us with many happy experiences that we will never forget as well as a comfortable home where we've spent many happy years Who could ask for more?

Mr. Vittitow's narrative names and describes the provenance of the shells, crystals, rocks and other unique specimens used to create the hearth. Photo by Gary Garson

Snyder : King House

The original construction of the King residence in Snyder (Scurry County) dates from the late 1800s. W.P. King Jr. was born in this house and as a boy in the '30s helped his father collect the stones and fossil wood which they used to expand and rock their home, where he lived until recently.

Brick soldier courses delineate and support door and window openings in walls of brightly colored stone and fossil wood in filled joint construction. The masonry was done by Frank Newby.

An undated King family photo of the home

Petrified wood logs surround a small backyard water feature.

The fireplace hearth was built by John Cole.

Northwestern Region 63

WESTERN REGION

About the geology

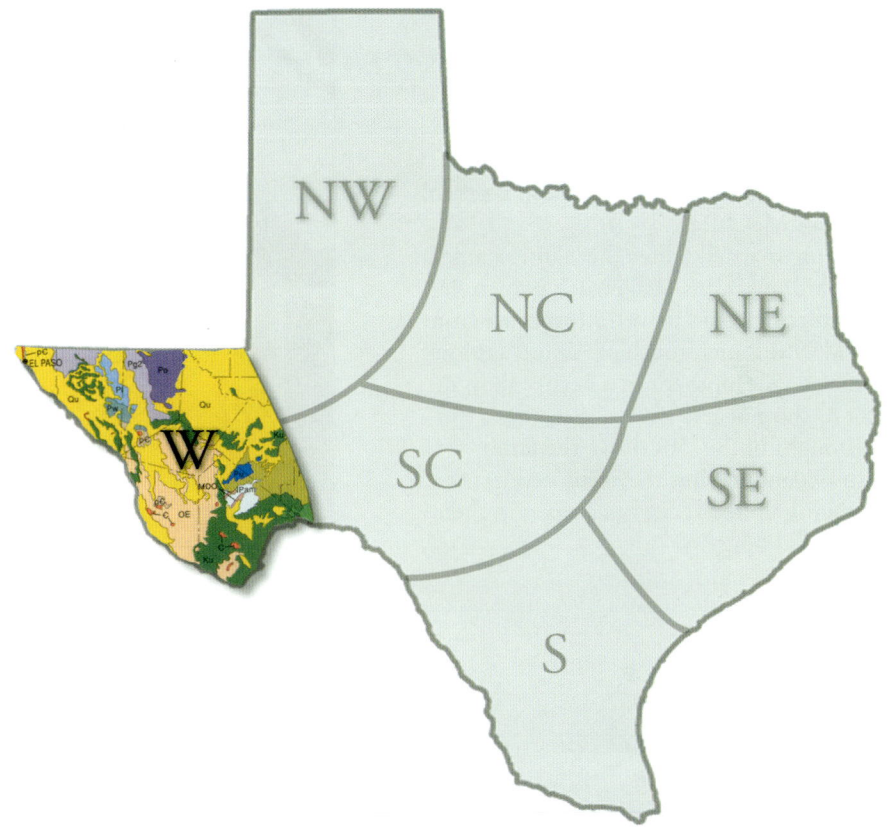

West Texas consists of an incredibly diverse mix of rock types – from Precambrian igneous, metamorphic, and sedimentary rocks to present day alluvium. This diversity is the result of two different mountain uplift episodes:

The first is the Marathon uplift of the Paleozoic Era (~300 m.y.) Ouachita Range from Marathon to the Big Bend on the southeastern part of West Texas. The second is the late Mesozoic Rocky Mountain uplift about 60 million years ago in the western portion of West Texas.

The final geologic episode was during the Tertiary Era (~35 m.y.) when extensive volcanism resulted in intrusive and extrusive basalt and ash layers throughout the region (Spearing, 1991).

During this period of time, the great Cretaceous interior seaway was becoming shallower and more restricted, progressively shifting eastward until disappearing altogether at the end of the Cretaceous (in conjunction with the Rocky Mountain uplift). The Big Bend area is the westernmost shore of that ancient sea, where the Aguja, the Javelina and the Paleocene Black Peaks formations were deposited between 80 and 55 million years ago.

Conditions were drier, but the area was still considered a lowland floodplain containing prolific amounts of dinosaur bone as well as fossilized trees. Most of the fossil occurrences are now located in the Big Bend National Park where collecting is prohibited.

Fossil animal and plant remains are so prevalent that fully or partially complete dinosaur skeletons have been excavated by academic and museum professionals for display and fossil wood has been sometimes used in construction. The fossil wood consists mostly of a wide variety of gymnosperm (conifer) families, but also contains some angiosperm (hardwood) species. This is noteworthy because the early Cretaceous is believed to be the time when angiosperms first evolved.

— *Scott Singleton*

Alpine: Walker House

Agnes Walker grew up in the house in Alpine (Brewster County). It was built in 1942 for her parents, Fred G. and Katheryn Walker, although she believes it was her grandfather, J.C. Walker, who funded construction costs for builder Matt McClure.

As a young married fellow, her father hauled the stone himself in his cattle truck (which he owned before he could drive). Most came from the Woodward Ranch south of Alpine, famous for its rocks. Her mother ran a beauty shop in one half of the garage.

The drought of the '50s drove the family north to Oklahoma, but they returned in the 1960s, taking up residence once again in their petrified wood house.

Fossil wood accents the multicolored sandstone veneer on the Walker House in Alpine.

A front view of the outbuilding used as a beauty shop

Petrified wood was used on the window sills of the beauty shop/garage.

66 • *Stone-Tree Houses of Texas*

This inlaid star mosaic can be seen in the background of the family photo at right.

All family photos courtesy of the Walker family

The Walker children were photographed in front of their West Texas rock house.

The fireplace is in a room added during a later expansion.

Western Region 67

Castolon: Dorgan House

The Albert (Bert) W. and Avis Dorgan house is located on a mesa near the settlement of Castolon in what is now Big Bend National Park and the Rancho Estelle Historic District. Known locally as an architect, Dorgan constructed an adobe house atop a mesa across from Santa Elena Canyon and overlooking the Rio Grande.

According to the notes from the Historical American Building Survey (HABS) Project in 1999, exact date of construction in the 1920s has not been established. For the place and time, it was a spacious 1,200-square-foot, four-room house with a large living area. The adobe walls and roof have succumbed to time, but the 10-foot-high, two-way petrified wood fireplace still stands at the center of the largest room. The "logs" of petrified wood mortared in lengthwise encase a 55-gallon barrel used as a liner; the fireplace supported four vigas, or ceiling beams, which extended to each corner of the living room.

The "Administrative History" of the park posits that Dorgan may have been the first to propose the idea of what would become Big Bend National Park; his map illustrating a "Friendly Nations Park" included land on both sides of the border; it is preserved in the Archives of the Big Bend in Alpine. He applied for a job with Harold Ickes, the secretary of the interior at the time, and included the map with his resume. His property became part of the national park. After leaving Texas, Dorgan apparently settled in Coral Gables, Fla., where he developed a plan for metropolitan Miami-Dade and established a Rotary Foundation scholarship to promote international peace.

The adobe house Bert Dorgan built in the 1920s near Castelon in the Big Bend area overlooked the Rio Grande. The mountains in the background above are in Mexico. The National Park Service has stabilized the remains of Bert Dorgan's adobe house and the 10-foot high two-way stone-tree fireplace still stands.

The Dorgan House as it looked in the early 1950s

All black and white photos courtesy of National Park Service at Big Bend National Park; Albert Dorgan's map, *International Peace Park*, courtesy of the Archives of the Big Bend in Alpine

A 1962 National Park Service survey photograph shows what remained at that time of large 'vigas' which once supported the roof.

Another National Park Service Survey image shows the large central fireplace

A drawing of the Dorgan House ruins from *The Journal of Big Bend Studies – From Castolon to Santa Elena: The People Behind the Ruins* by artist Susan Tanner, courtesy of the Big Bend Natural History Association

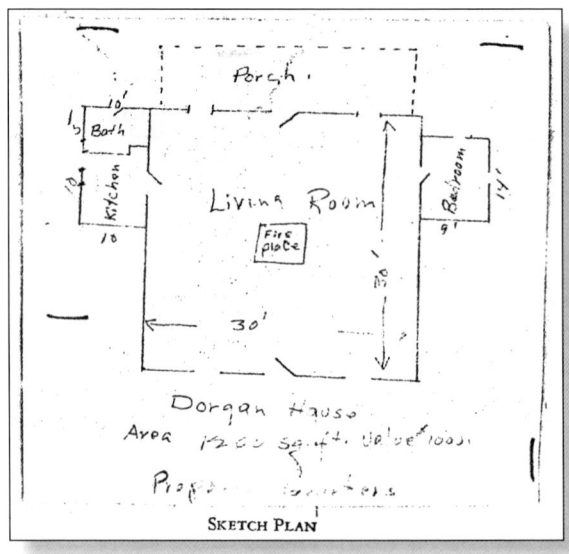

A field sketch from the National Park Service shows the layout of the Dorgan house and notes the approximate area as 1,200 square feet and gives a value of $1,000.

Mr. Dorgan's 1938 hand-rendered map of the nation's major parks includes his proposed location for an International Peace Park incorporating lands on both sides of the Mexico-Texas border in the Big Bend area. Part of Mr. Dorgan's dream has come to pass — Big Bend National Park was created in 1944, and Mexico and the United States met in 2010 to discuss designating the Big Bend — Rio Bravo as a natural area of binational interest.

North Central Region

About the Geology

The western two-thirds of this region is dominated by red Permian and Pennsylvanian sediments laid down in an arid environment on the edge of the great Permian Basin further to the southwest.

During the Cretaceous when the inland seaway was active, thick sequences of carbonate rocks were deposited on top of the Permian and Pennsylvanian sediments. However, with the uplift of the Rocky Mountains these Cretaceous sediments have been progressively removed and transported to the Gulf of Mexico (Spearing, 1991).

At the present day, the remnants of the thick Cretaceous limestones lie on the eastern portions of this region. Because they are hard rocks that are resistive to erosion, they tend to form bluffs where they still exist.

As the inland seaway was progressively opening in the early Cretaceous, transgressive sheet sands were deposited near the coastline. These sheet sands moved with the coastline back and forth as the sea levels rose unevenly, sometimes regressing completely to the shelf edge near the present day Gulf of Mexico only to move back over the land surface as the sea level rose again.

By the end of the early Cretaceous, the seas were at their highest where they remained through most of the last half of the Cretaceous. It was during these times that the thick sequences of limestones were deposited.

The transgressive sheet sands of the early Cretaceous preserved a large variety of plant and animal remains.

The famous dinosaur tracks of the Glen Rose Formation are but one example. Dinosaur bones have been excavated from a number of locations in central and north-central Texas.

Petrified wood is also common in these sediments. The formations that contain fossils of land-based life forms are collectively known as the Trinity Group (Sellards, 1932; ~108-130 m.y.). Specifically within this group of formations are the Twin Mountains Formation, Travis Peak Formation, Paluxy Sand, and Antlers Sand, along with the more famous Glen Rose Limestone which does not generally contain fossil wood (Barnes, 1992).

Preservation is generally not good in these early Cretaceous fossil woods. However, they are so prevalent where they outcrop that it is relatively common to see them used as construction material. A notable example is in the city of Glen Rose which is well known for the large number of houses and walls built with the material.

— *Scott Singleton*

Decatur: Texas Tourist Camp

The complex known as the Texas Tourist Camp began as two wooden structures, a gas station and a café, built by E.F. Boydston in 1927 on the corner of U.S. 380 and U.S. 287 in Decatur (Wise County) to serve the growing number of motorists traveling through the area. (He allowed the travelers to build campfires.)

Additional structures were added over the next few years and in 1935 when the highway was widened, his brother Nolan covered the original wooden buildings with petrified wood collected from around Alvord and Bridgeport.

The Boydston family operated the Texas Lunchroom, later renamed The Texas Café, until it closed in 1988. Since then Mr. Boydston's granddaughter Nancy Rosendahl and her husband Jim have restored the complex, reopening the cafe in 1993, turning the station into a private office, and refurbishing the motel rooms. Lunch is again being served in what is now called the Whistle Stop Café.

Bonnie Parker and Clyde Barrow are said to have spent a few nights at the tourist camp during their 1930s crime spree. And, in another claim to fame, award-winning country artist Faith Hill used the motel as a set in 2001 when she recorded "There You'll Be" for the movie *Pearl Harbor*, and stayed in Bonnie's room.

Texas Tourist Camp remains one of a few examples of tourist courts built throughout Texas following the expansion of roads supported by the National Highway Act. The buildings were placed on the National Register of Historic Places in 1997.

Black and white photos courtesy of Nancy and Jim Rosendahl and the National Register of Historic Places

A 1953 aerial photograph of the Texas Tourist Camp Complex

Nolan Boydston helps a customer in this 1945 photo; recapping tires was good business in the 1940s. The cabins in the back were not yet rocked.

The Texas Tourist Camp in Decatur is one of a few surviving examples of tourist courts built throughout Texas following the expansion of roads in the 1920s under the National Highway Act. The buildings in the complex were placed on the National Register of Historic Places in 1997.

Wrapped in neon during the 1930s, the now restored Petrified Wood Station and Texas Plaza once again beckons road-weary travelers.

Jacksboro: Nash House

An old family photo of the Nash House

Mr. W.L. Nash

Nature has invaded the remains of Mr. Nash's store across the street from his home. The store sold gas and groceries but was closed when the highway was widened, leaving no room for the gas pumps.

William Lee Nash, a local grocer and later the owner of the local hardware store, built this home for himself with the help of one other man; neither was a professional mason. It is believed that the fossil wood used in the home came from around the Glen Rose area. Stylistically, the house is similar to many buildings in Glen Rose.

Directly across the road and similar in appearance to his own house, Nash also built an early "convenience store," incorporating petrified wood, sandstone, limestone and pieces of green slag glass. The store, now a ruin, sold gas and groceries and had a meat and cheese market at the back. The property also included four small cabins of similar stone construction with connecting garages available for rental.

Black and white photos courtesy of the Nash family.

A closer look at the chimney

Schnieder/Burger House

Paul Schnieder, who operated a bait, hamburger and gasoline business on site, built this small rectangular-plan house west of Fort Worth (Tarrant County). The 1986 Historical Resources Survey states that this building exemplifies the petrified wood and stone construction used during the '30s to evoke a rustic image in the Tudor Revival style. Hugo and Gladys Burger, operators of adjacent Burger's Lake, owned the home from 1937 to 1964.

Petrified wood covers almost 100 percent of the exterior.

Petrified wood pieces fill the twin-gables of an entry to the Schnieder/Burger House.

Schnieder/Burger House

A side view shows one of two large fossil wood chimneys.

Fossil ammonites line a walkway.

Massive logs of petrified wood were used to rock the two chimneys.

86 • *Stone-Tree Houses of Texas*

O.D. Stevens House

A newspaper story reveals that Mr. Stevens made no secret of his involvement in bootlegging but hid his narcotics trafficking. His neighbors regarded him as a 'square shooter' who kept his word and paid his debts with cash peeled from a large roll of bills.

'Mystery House'

O. D. Stevens built this large stone veneer house in 1933. Soon after it was built, Stevens was convicted for his part in the robbery of $71,000 from the Fort Worth Texas and Pacific Railroad Station. He was also convicted of murdering three of his accomplices in the robbery after an argument over the loot, but was subsequently acquitted on retrial. Stevens was eventually sentenced to 27 years in prison for the robbery and served time in Alcatraz and Leavenworth before being paroled in 1950. Stevens' accomplice, W. D. May, was convicted and executed for the murders.

The Stevens house was designed as a hideout, with many secret rooms and compartments. Reportedly he used only outside labor so no one locally would know the house's hiding places. One room is accessible only by lifting up the main stairs. Another can be reached only through an exterior dormer window. Federal agents found over $100,000 in narcotics hidden in the house after Stevens' arrest and there is speculation that half the stolen $71,000 never recovered by the T&P Railroad may still be hidden in the house.

The house has passed through several owners since Stevens was convicted. During the 1940s the house was a rest home, but returned to use as a private home in the 1950s and '60s. In 1981 the house was remodeled as a restaurant. It soon closed and the house remained vacant until being repurposed as a day care center.

According to notes in the 1986 Fort Worth Historical Resources Survey, the house is a larger more elaborate version of a stone veneer, Period Revival house popular in Fort Worth during the 1930s. Faced in fine sandstone with limestone quoins and window surrounds, the house has two steeply pitched gables which intersect the main cross gable. The main entrance portico has a round arch opening with a richly textured surround faced with narrow pieces of petrified wood. A wide hipped roof covers with front entrance porch which wraps around from the front to the south elevations. The main front gable has a flaring side eave which shelters a narrow round arch portico.

Newspaper clippings courtesy of the Fort Worth Star-Telegram

In 1933, O.D. Stevens was implicated as the mastermind of a postal robbery of the Texas and Pacific Rail Station and the subsequent triple murder of members of his gang in a dispute over the loot. Stevens had the men killed, wrapped in fence wire, weighted with cement and dumped into the Trinity River. The bodies surfaced and the trail soon led back to Stevens. Police searching the home for evidence in the murder soon found numerous secret compartments built into the home and eventually uncovered a large cache of narcotics and other evidence indicating Stevens' participation in a variety of criminal enterprises. The story created a media sensation with lurid details documented in the local press.

TRAP DOOR FLIES OPEN AS OFFICERS PULL SASH CORDS

House of Mystery Outrivals Wildest Crime Wizardry of Screen

Mansion on Hilltop Outside Handley Might Be Setting for Thriller Greater Than Edgar Wallace Ever Wrote

Within the last four days the story of an epic of crime has suddenly been laid out before the public of Fort Worth and the Southwest.

Unwinding in mysterious detail, it outrivals the wildest crime wizardry of the screen, and out-shrieks the imagination of an Edgar Wallace.

A farm mansion sitting quietly behind its mask of trees in the summer sunshine is revealed as a house of mystery which may hold the key to the fate of three missing men.

Its owner, O. D. Stevens, whose quietly sinister air daunted his neighbors, who has gone about his own mysterious business behind a mask of secrecy, is in the county jail formally charged with murder, with narcotic possession, and with taking part in the $72,000 mail robbery in Fort Worth last February.

He is praised by some neighbors for his generosity, while his ruthless air daunted others.

That $72,000 robbery at one time threatened to go down in the history of the U. S. mails as an unsolved crime.

To what others may the quiet mansion at Handley hold the key? What other dark transactions may have been planned or completed behind its walls?

Already the 'House of Mystery's' secret panels and swinging stairs have given up the biggest cache of narcotics ever seized in Fort Worth, solving the robbery of a drug store in Waco a month ago.

What of the three missing men —Jack Sturdivant, Eula; J. B. Rutherford, Dallas, and Harry H. Rutherford, Abilene?

Did they purposely plant bloodstained, bullet-pierced old clothes in the crude hog-wire basket in the Trinity, and slip into a new life in a new country as quietly as they escaped with the mail loot?

Some believe they got their share of the spoils and are now many hundreds of miles from here to begin a new life. If so, why did they do it in a way sure to bring the bloodhounds of the law upon the trail? Why did the mother of two of them sob and almost faint when the clothing was shown to her?

The car in which the three men left Dallas and in which they were last seen has never been found. No trace of the men has been found in the "House of Mystery" nor in the woods and streams nearby.

Does Stevens, alleged dope peddler and alleged brains of a dope and robbery gang—our man of mystery in this exciting drama—hold the key to the whole thing?

Were the men murdered when they came to demand their $9,000 share of the loot from the $72,000 postal robbery?

Is their car standing in the deep waters of some river, or lake, with three nude and bullet-pierced bodies still in it? Or what significance may there be in the quoted remark of Stevens

(Turn to Page 7).

MYSTERY HOUSE LIKE THRILLER

Bares Crimes As Startling As Wildest Tales Of Edgar Wallace

(Starts on Page 1).

about how he disposed of his foes?

To this major mystery the city and county police forces, and the crew of federal narcotic operatives brought in from the entire Southwest, have found no answer.

So far as the fate of the missing men is concerned, they are no further than they were when they started Sunday with discovery of the wire-bound clothing.

Stevens, a man with a family of three children, was almost as much a mystery to his family as to his neighbors.

His sister, Miss Fay Stevens, a frail Osceola, Ark., school teacher who came to the Stevens country home "for a rest," hysterically told officers she knew nothing of Stevens and his business. First held, she has been released. Her vacation has turned into a nightmare.

Innocent Victims.

The wife and three children profess to be equally as ignorant of secret niches and panels. The latter, one 17 and ill, one 15 and one 14, are the innocent victims of the whole tragedy.

The beautiful red sandstone mansion that commands the crest of a hill near Handley was not built on the bare returns from a small patch of peanuts and peas, now taken by the weeds.

The house was begun last fall but was not completed and occupied until two months ago—the work mostly done by labor foreign to this section. The postal robbery was staged during the interval.

The house is the last word in modern building achievement. There are beautifully tinted walls, shower baths, indirect lighting systems and the most elaborate of furnishings.

Also Builds House.

W. D. May, a neighbor, also charged in the murder, had begun a like mansion on 50 acres deeded to him by Stevens. Only the foundation had been completed. Where did the money come from?

According to the story given officers, the three missing men staged the robbery while Stevens and others waited in a cafe across Lancaster Avenue.

Stevens, it is asserted, planned the whole thing and frequented the cafes near the new U. S. postoffice where postal employes eat. In this way from overhearing conversations he learned how and when important money bags were shipped.

Otherwise, how could seven bags containing big money have been picked from 50, in such a quick and efficient manner?

Stevens then took the loot to New York, exchanged it for other bills and returned, the officers assert.

The missing trio never got their $9,000 share, it was said. They had gone to demand it when they disappeared.

A police investigator demonstrates a secret panel activated by pulling a sash cord. Secret panels were found throughout the O.D. Stevens' residence and in the homes of his associates.

As Suspects' Wives Were Taken to Criminal Court Building

This snapshot was taken Thursday morning as the wives of two of the defendants in the triple slaying were being taken from the courthouse to the Criminal Court Building. Left to right, Deputy Sheriff Ralph Martin, Mrs. W. D. May, who is charged with vagrancy; Mrs. O. D. Stevens, who is held on a narcotic charge, ney Clyde Mays. In the center is Attorney Charles

Above and right, an article speculates on the fate of the three missing members of the Stevens' gang and describes the home as 'the last word in modern building achievement.'

O. D. Stevens Termed Mail Robbery 'Mind'

The wives of the gangsters, Mrs. W.D. May, left, and Mrs. O.D. Stevens, and their attorneys enter the court building.

BIG NARCOTIC CACHE FOUND IN HOUSE

A map with an 'X' marking the location where a wire bundle containing bloodstained clothing of the three missing men was found.

The hardscaping of O.D. Stevens' Hadley residence featured a half-circle of fieldstone stairs leading to gabled front entrance and a surrounding wall.

Stevens Commercial Building

Contractor V.L. Pursely used sandstone and petrified wood to construct a building for O.D. Stevens on a visually prominent corner in the commercial area of the Handley District (Tarrant County). These were popular exterior materials for houses during the 1930s, but rarely used for commercial buildings. The fossil wood frieze along the parapet and the varying shades of sandstone draw attention to a unique building. A drugstore has occupied the property since 1933. Sold in 1934, it passed through several owners until the family of the current owners purchased it in 1942. Its distinctive look contributed to Central Handley being named a National Register Historic District.

A frieze atop of the walls features a pattern of smaller pieces of petrified wood.

Sandstone and petrified wood cover the O.D. Stevens building.

North Central Region

Colleyville: Black House

'Rockwood Farm'

According to their descendants, the John Rollo and Ruth (Drydere) Black house was originally part of "Rockwood Farm," which included several hundred acres and a pond in Colleyville (Tarrant County).

In 1933, Black hired local stonemason Walter Reynolds to assist him in the rocking in of an existing building with petrified wood. Laying the stone as Black's Scottish ancestors taught him, the masons mixed concrete in a wheelbarrow, not too much at a time, chose thick rocks and used a trowel to scrape the joints out for the look they wanted.

The house is generally rectangular in plan, with a transverse front gable; there were three bedrooms, a large bath, and a full basement; the screened in sleeping porch and a swimming pool were added later. They also built a house for the sharecroppers.

John R. Black practiced law and served as a judge in Tarrant County; he also helped incorporate Colleyville.

Black and white photos courtesy of Lori Black Johnson

The John R. Black House at Colleyville

This petrified wood doghouse no longer stands. It is one of two found in this book (see pg. 187).

North Central Region 93

The chimney of the John R. Black House

Outbuildings and features then and now include a ' summer kitchen' (top), a small stone shed (center) and a well (bottom).

Stonemason Walter Reynolds

According to the *Tarrant County History*, after stonemason Walter Reynolds married in 1914, he purchased a 63-acre farm on Pleasant Run Road.

The abundance of native stones he found while working his land as well as his interest in them led him to build his first stone house which he rented out for additional income.

After his first wife died, Mr. Reynolds married longtime friend Sylvia Barclay and, in what is believed to be a first for women in Texas, taught her masonry. The couple veneered houses throughout the area with native stone found in Colleyville or picked and hauled by hand from neighboring counties.

The account states that, "Walter cut and placed the rock on the exterior of a house, Sylvia put a beautiful finishing touch with her trowel, sealing each stone in a raised seam around it." Many older homes were spared demolition because the Reynolds "rocked" the house.

Walter Reynolds, here in front of the first house he rocked, taught his wife to lay stone.

North Central Region

Gordon : Ringo Ranch

The 'Bar J' design laid into the chimney of this 1939 house some miles outside of Gordon (Palo Pinto County) remains a mystery, especially to the family members who have never found a connection to the builders of the house, Ross and Margaret Murl (Maddox) Ringo. Mrs. Ringo drew up the plans for the three-bedroom house that featured a cistern for water, a full basement, and a T-shaped upstairs.

Their granddaughter remembers that there were no electric lines – she still has the cases for the batteries which powered the appliances in the house – and says that her grandfather himself dug the holes for the telephones poles. She also can remember her mother sliding around on top of the house, helping to put on the panels for a new roof. Petrified rocks were also used to create curved flower beds around the house.

Ross and Margaret Murl Ringo

The tree in the foreground of an early photo now shades the brick-lined arches of the Ringo House.

The Ringo House construction included such details as the stacked fossil wood pieces which cap the chimney and stone 'faces' laid into a garage wall.

The niche in the chimney was a popular design element.

Black and white photos courtesy of the Ringo family

North Central Region 97

ABILENE : SHOEMAKER HOUSE

The Hart and Rebecca Shoemaker House on the banks of Elm Creek in Abilene (Taylor County) was built about 1938. According to their daughter, her dad loved rocks and recalls that when her dad and mother returned from a trip, the car would be filled with "fancy" rocks. She believes that the petrified wood came from around DeLeon and Gorman and that the mason was Albert McAlister. The Shoemaker House remained in the family and is today an Abilene Historic Landmark.

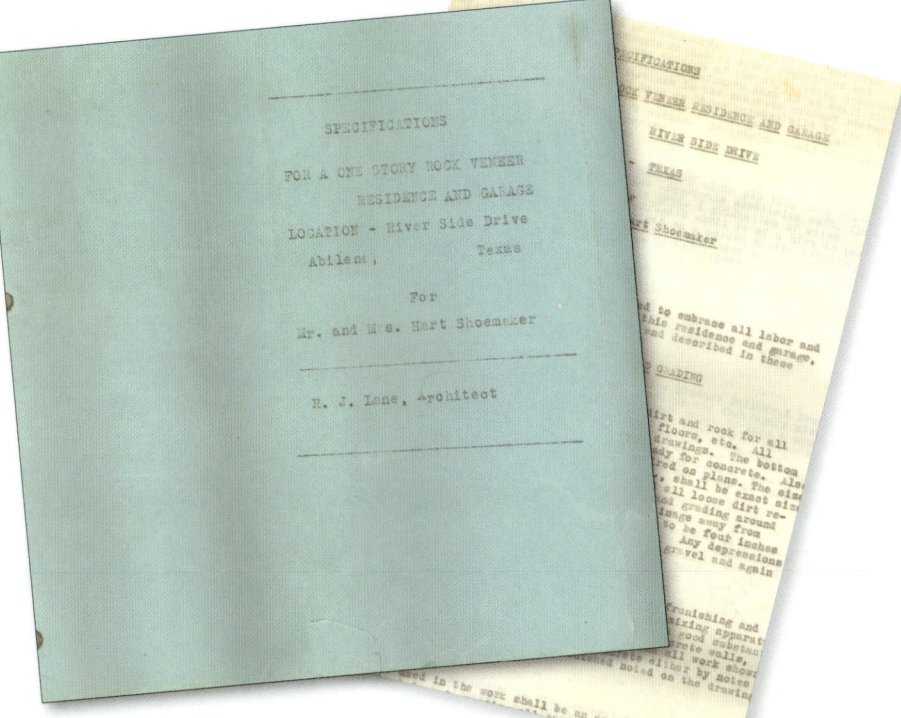

The family kept a copy of the specifications of architect R.J. Lane for the rock-veneer, one-story house. (See Appendix F, pg.266)

Black and white photos and archival materials courtesy of the Shoemaker family

'Fancy' stones and a mantel of granite (probably from Marble Falls) decorate the fireplace in the Shoemaker House. The arc of the hearth was formed with fossil wood and granite.

Fossils, quartz crystals, petrified wood and unusual stones frame a pond.

North Central Region

Rebecca Shoemaker (at right) and her daughter Freelin shared a moment in a part of the backyard above Elm Creek that the family called the "second bank." A fireplace and chimney were built into a rock wall extending up the hill.

Highly polychromatic, unusual and decorative specimen stones compliment pieces of petrified wood inlaid in a niche on the chimney.

A large metal hook inside the outdoor hearth supported large iron pots.

At left above, a front view of the Shoemaker House from the 1930s and on the right, from 2007

The home bears an Abilene Historic Landmark plaque.

A newspaper ad for Mr. Shoemaker's car lot and insurance agency shows that his downtown office building was also built with fossil wood.

Glen Rose

Young's Service Station just outside Glen Rose hints at the city's wealth of stone tree houses, buildings and architectural features that gave 'The Petrified City' its nickname.

**Black and white photos courtesy of
Dorothy Leach and the Somervell County Historical Society**

Sycamore Grove

Built in 1928 by stonemason Gran Norman, the walls of this distinctive structure still stand on the outskirts of Glen Rose at a fork in the road known locally as 'Sycamore Grove.'

Young's Service Station was originally a gas station and garage and later housed other businesses, including a speakeasy during Prohibition.

It was one of the few buildings constructed almost entirely of petrified wood and solid masonry. Intricate inlays of large fossil logs and other architectural details attest to the mason's artistry and skill.

North Central Region 103

'The Petrified City'

Located in Somervell County's scenic Paluxy River Valley in North Central Texas, the history of Glen Rose is as colorful as the fossilized wood that permeates the region. Studies of the geology and fossils indicate that a mostly coniferous forest flourished on the plains that bordered the waters of the ancient sea which 110 million years ago covered the eastern curve of what is now the Texas coastline.

First settled about 1860, the town was founded around a gristmill and grew into a regional trade center. After the turn of the century, natural mineral springs drew a variety of healers and their clients to "take the waters" in a town bejeweled with glittering rocks.

Other curious visitors wanted to see dinosaur tracks discovered in 1908 in the limestone of the river bottom. The advent of the automobile and improved roads in the '20s brought yet more traffic. A flood of bootleggers during Prohibition earned 'The Petrified City' another nickname – "Moonshine Capital of Texas."

It was during this era that it became fashionable to cover existing or new homes and buildings with a veneer of the attractive, inexpensive and abundant petrified wood easily procured from farmers glad to have it out of their fields. They would pile it along their fence lines, charging only a few dollars a truckload to those who would haul it away. These stones were used more extensively in the construction of buildings in Glen Rose than anywhere else in Texas and although many no longer stand, it is believed that at one time there were as many as 50 such structures.

J.W. Davis of Dublin, now in his 80s, remembers carrying cement as a boy in the '30s for his dad and granddad, both stonemasons. Mr. Davis believes that the workers hired to help lay the rocks were paid according to the number of stones they laid. Other sources say that the masons earned $1 a day, the helpers 50 cents.

"My dad worked at Glen Rose right outside of town before I was born in 1928. He built the cottages in the little park by the river [Rivercrest Park] – the older ones, not the newer ones – you can tell the difference – and the swimming pool and probably the arch over the entrance to River Crest and the gas station there on Bernard Street."

Historic Town Square

A variety of restaurants, stores and curiosity shops prospered for a time in Glen Rose. Tom's Cabin, a roadside eatery catering to the newly mobile tourist trade, once stood near the town square and featured the colorful agatized façade popular in the 1920s and '30s. A small sign in the window advertises 'petrified wood for s[ale].'

A mixture of fossil wood on the bandstand in the town square surrounds a Mesozoic-Era dinosaur track excavated from what is now called the Paluxy River Dinosaur Trackway. A petrified knothole is part of the mix.

A star-shaped fountain rimmed with petrified wood is part of the courthouse square hardscaping.

A plaque on the gazebo lists the contractor as G.M. Sellars and the date of construction in 1933.

North Central Region 105

Milling Sanitarium

The Milling Sanitarium on Bernard Street was built in 1910 as a retreat. The veneer on first floor walls is almost entirely of petrified wood; a second floor in brick was added in the '30s. When the magnetic healer Dr. Roscoe G. Milling owned the property, he added several more petrified wood buildings. His son, R. G. Milling Jr., continued to operate the sanitarium until 1962. Repurposed as the Hotel Carlsbad, later renamed the Shady Inn, and later yet operated as an antique mall, the building has been restored recently and reopened as the Bernard St. Cottages.

Snyder House

Dr. George P. 'Doc' Snyder and his wife Maggie built this retreat with petrified wood and colorful local stone in 1929 at the edge of Glen Rose.

Lane's Ford Agency

Now unoccupied but still intact, the petrified wood rock on Lane's Ford Agency and Garage near the square was laid by stonemason Gran Norman, who reportedly also rocked many of the other building façades in Glen Rose. According to Dorothy Leach of the Somervell County Historical Commission, other workmen on the structure were Peavine Ramsay, John Taylor, John Cinto, and Tobe Keenum; the rock came from the Leslie Hart farm in the Rock Creek Community.

Fire Station/City Hall

Designed originally as a fire station, the petrified wood and limestone building was repurposed many times over the years, even serving for a time as Glen Rose City Hall.

Marsh House

The 'Honeymoon Cottage' dates from the early 1930s.

Known as the 'Honeymoon Cottage,' local historians say that Wesley Marsh borrowed $1,400 from a 'magnetic healer' to finance this unique petrified wood present for his bride-to-be, Marvin Morton. A trucker by trade, Marsh hauled the wood from Hood County. Reportedly, the local builder was F.S. Williams, with the masonry work supervised by Roy English (who also built the Pressley House (pg. 172) in Hoyte. A member of the family remembers that Mrs. Marsh was especially pleased because her new two-bedroom home had a bathtub and a commode, 'the most beautiful thing,' and one of the first stoves in Glen Rose that didn't need wood.

Photos courtesy of Woodard family descendants and the Somervell County Historical Commission.

Wes Marsh (above) also helped his brother-in-law, John Woodard, truck tons of petrified wood from Glen Rose in 1935 to build the Petrified Forest Lodge (pg. 154) on what is now Guadalupe Street in Austin.

Wes Marsh (at left) helped mix cement in front of the partially finished façade.

Gresham House

Later owner Erma Moore Blackstock believed that it was masons Frank McCoy, Gran Norman, and Wheeler Nabors who built this house on the banks of the Paluxy for Lewis and Ima Lou Gresham in 1929. The walls of the classic bungalow-style house are covered with a complex veneer of fossil wood from the Rock Creek area and fieldstone trimmed in brick. A photo taken around the time of its completion shows that later remodeling altered some of the original woodwork.

Pruitt House

The two stone-tree columns on the porch and the large fossil wood and native stone pieces used to face the wood frame structure distinguish W.B. Pruitt's bungalow.

The name, 'Dr. W.B. Pruitt,' spelled out at the entrance to the porch identifies the original owner.

At right, a mosaic of smooth river rocks inlaid with smaller pieces of petrified wood, details the chimney.

Stephenville: Wolfe Nursery

Pioneer horticulturist Ross R. Wolfe and his wife Mabel founded their nursery in 1919 on 12 acres west of Stephenville (Erath County) as a "Mom and Pop" enterprise, specializing in pecan trees.

The Wolfes themselves collected many of the stone-tree rocks and fossils used to construct the distinctive offices which, along with plants and animals at the nursery, became a well-known landmark and tourist attraction in Texas and beyond, even catching the attention of "Ripley's Believe It or Not."

Hugh Wolfe, son of Ross Wolfe and also a savvy businessman, always sought new ways to market his products – first embracing "mail order" and later becoming one of the first to appreciate the power of radio advertising and to utilize the new medium aggressively. Wolfe Nursery grew into a premier supplier of plants in the United States.

Porch and archway of the nursery office

The Wolf Nursery, completed in 1929, was Texas landmark for more than 75 years.

Color photos courtesy of Joyce Whitis

These two black and white images were found in the San Antonio home of Monroe Nowotny (pg. 236).

110 • *Stone-Tree Houses of Texas*

Joyce Whitis of Stephenville wrote this article on the Wolf Nursery about 1990.

'The House that Time Built'

The little house is a source of fascination for the average person traveling down far West Washington Street. Standing close up to the curb, at the point where Wolfe Nursery Road takes off beside the Super Wal-Mart Center to join up with North West Loop, the house of unusual construction is a traffic stopper.

For the recreational rock hound and serious geologist, this particular piece of architecture is a sight to warm the heart.

Drive in and park. Walk up the front steps ending at a locked door. Stand there for a few minutes and examine the walls. There's a dinosaur track, cut out of solid rock on the Paluxy River and now part of the front porch. Over there on that wall, there's an absolutely perfect ammonite, twelve inches in diameter. As the visitor's fingers touch the shell of an ancestor to the snail that lived in the Jurassic age, the mind spins in wonder that one man in his lifetime could collect all this marvelous display of ancient history.

"Serpent stones" these petrified creatures were called by early naturalists but actually they are common invertebrate shell fossils. They lived and then died some 60 million years ago.

Ripley once featured this remarkable building, constructed in 1929, in his *Believe It or Not* strip and called it the "House that Time Built." Looking at the countless petrified wood, stalactites, a cavity of crystals from inside an ammonite, and most rare of all cycads, ancient plants dating back to the Devonian and Carboniferous ages.

"Dad found a patch of those cycads (a piece of petrified wood that mostly resembles a large tree root) south of town, said Hugh Wolfe, son of Wolfe Nursery founder, Ross Wolfe. He called a friend, Dr. Wayland from Yale University who took two of the fossils back to Yale and gave one to the Smithsonian."

Wolfe looked up toward a small window in the old building. "See there's one on each side of that window."

Lots of folks in their 60s and 70s, who lived in other places around the state, remember Wolfe Nursery radio ads as their first recognition of Stephenville.

"My mother used to order pecan trees from Wolfe's and tomatoes from Porter," an older woman remarked.

"I remember the ads on the radio. That's one of the first things I remember hearing, ads from Wolfe Nursery in Stephenville," her husband said.

"Those ads got me in real trouble too," Wolfe remarked. "During 1938 I saw the value of radio advertising. I was guest on a sports show that made a big chain of men's stores throughout California.

After I saw what radio ads could do, I made a deal with Carr P. Collins in Dallas to sell small "Home Orchards" through the powerful radio stations in Mexico. We used the famous Stamps Quartet and orders for the $1.98 orchard delivered, swamped us.

The package included five peach trees, one apple, one plum, 25 strawberry, and 10 blackberry plants.

"Our annual sales exploded from $60,000 to over one million in just one year. Overnight the Stephenville Post Office grew from 3rd to 1st class. Stephenville and Wolfe Nursery were on the map. The only problem was, we were just not equipped to handle this kind of sales

Ross and Mabel Wolfe

An 'S' is formed with fossilized ammonites set into the petrified wood.

Hugh Wolfe, son of Ross and Mabel Wolfe, passed away in 2010 at the age of 97.

An aerial view of Wolfe Nursery property shows the little stone house fronting U.S. 377. Photo courtesy of Tarleton State University.

Cars crowded the nursery parking lot on a busy sale day. When the Wolfes invited the public onto the grounds for a special occasion, noted a Wolfe descendant, 'They came from as far away as Merkel.'

Office of Wolfe's Pecan Nursery - Stephenville, Texas.
Made of Petrified Wood and Fossils.

THE HOUSE THAT TIME BUILT

OFFICE: WOLFE'S NURSERY — STEPHENVILLE, TEXAS — MADE OF PETRIFIED WOOD AND FOSSILS

was up and running big time.

What an long way they had come.

Ross R. Wolfe and Mabel Ida Tanner were married in 1911 in a small church near the Pedernales River.

The newly married couple moved to Mason, where they farmed and Ross taught school in a rural one room school house. In 1914 they moved to California where Ross worked as a mail carrier.

One day he met Luther Burbank who changed the course of the young Wolfe family's future.

"If I were a young man, I would move to Texas and develop a Pecan Nursery," Burbank told Wolfe.

The Wolfes came back to Texas and he took a job as a traveling salesman for the Waxahachie Nursery Company. After getting together a small "grubstake," the family bought 60 acres of sandy land two miles west of Stephenville. The year was 1919, and Wolfe Pecan Nursery was founded on a choice five-acre parcel of land.

There were two boys, Hugh and Danny, and four girls, Billie, Erma, Virginia, and Sybil and times were hard. Hugh remembers how his mother cried when they moved into an old house north of Highway 377. That became their home place for 68 years but when they first had to clear brush to reach the house that had not one whole window pane in it, Mrs. Wolfe just buried her face in her hands.

"Dad worked the nursery during the summer and traveled during winter, mother took care of us six kids, picked cotton for the neighbors and handled all of the office work. Money was hard to come by and Dad would take nearly anything in trade for pecan trees. We were loaded with hogs, goats, cows, horses, mules and chickens," Wolfe remembered.

As the nursery grew in size and reputation, pecan trees were shipped to several countries in the free world. Such slogans as, "The sun never sets on Wolfe grown pecan trees," and "Money does grow on trees" became common. Hugh Wolfe, of an artistic nature, designed the famous sign that stood on top of the home sales building for many years. It was of a wolf, pocket bulging with money, eyes gleaming as he counted his bills. Ross Wolfe died

volume."

Ross Wolfe called in the George S. May Company in Chicago to do a complete management engineering overhaul of the nursery operations. They overhauled the company and gave lessons in business management at the same time.

Major improvements in all departments of the nursery were made.

Wolfe Nursery developed the first mechanical pecan tree digger that cut costs 80 percent over iron-handle shovel digging that often damaged the root system.

They installed a drip-irrigation system and cut out unprofitable production. Wolfe Nursery in Stephenville

a painful death from cancer in 1948, two and half years after his doctor gave him six months to live. He was responsible for making this world a better place because of his knowledge and his dedicated hard work.

He introduced Vetch (a legume soil builder) to Erath County, and pecan trees to the world. He promoted highways, bridges, soil conservation, Tarleton and public schools. He was one of three men who purchased and gave Memorial Stadium and Wisdom Gym to Tarleton and was a major influence in getting the Texas A&M Experiment Station located in Stephenville.

Ross Wolfe was a rockhound and an amateur geologist. He loved to talk fossils and rocks and in his travels around the country, always picked up and brought back a few "rocks" that were of interest to him.

Thus in 1929 he designed and built the one-of-a-kind office for Wolfe Nursery. This building is truly a building that time built. It took centuries to form the magnificent rocks and fossilized creatures that compose this building. An interested person can spend hours examining the walls and always there is something new, something that hadn't been noticed before. The fireplace inside is also constructed of age old rock.

This unique building is one of Stephenville's most valuable treasures, a tribute to the man who built it and the business that helped put Stephenville on the map.

It took millions of years to form the material from which this house is made. Hopefully it will stand as a monument for many generations to enjoy. There is nothing else left of what once was a major business in this part of the country.

The familiar Wolf, the sign designed by Hugh that became a landmark, is packed away in storage. It belongs to the city of Stephenville whose governing body seems unsure what to do with it. The land on which the nursery stood, including the unique house, is for sale. The fate of the sign, the future of the house that time built, and the history that clings to them both, will be decided by others.

THE WOLFE NURSERY BUILDING WAS DEMOLISHED ABOUT 1991.

History takes a tumble Friday as crews demolish the historic Wolfe Nursery home on the corner of Wolfe Nursery Road and U.S. 377. The demolition was ordered by the property owners, who live outside of Erath County. The activity resulted in numerous calls to Brooks Real Estate objecting to the action.

BIG BAD WOLFE
A Disney concept designed by Hugh Wolfe stood above the WOLFE NURSERY sign 45 years. Known and loved far and wide. Made by the Dallas Sign Co. that made Magnolia's Flying Horse. Wolfe motto "Money Does Grow On Trees"

The nursery's trademark sign was designed by son Hugh Wolfe, who later donated it to the Stephenville Museum.

North Central Region

Latham House

Descendants of Millard Lee and Middie Mae (Martin) Latham have preserved in a family history the story of the Latham home in Stephenville (Erath County).

Mr. Latham, according to his doctor, needed fresh air and exercise, so rock hauling became his cure. For years, he made arrangements with landowners to lease land outside of Stephenville, where he and his boys cleared fields and creek bottoms, gathering large stones to fill the lot he had purchased in town. Their history notes the patience and diligence he and the boys displayed in their rock hunting (someone always won the weight-lifting contest). On Sundays, it was a family excursion, with his wife and daughters also helping.

The documents credit Mr. Latham with the drawing of the floor plan and name Hubert and Cecil Darby as builders (with Mr. Latham's approval before any rock was tapped into place). The masons started with the walls outside and the flowerbeds around the parameters and used the same forms used for the dorms at Tarleton State. All the interior walls were solid wood. Mr. Latham also designed the fireplace with its red floor, which was lined with white bricks, and objected if anyone wanted to actually light a fire in it. The family moved in, new furniture and all, in 1936.

After the Lathams passed away, the house was sold and became a daycare for a while. Years later, a granddaughter wanted to return to Stephenville and was looking for a house to buy; when she learned her grandparents' place was on the market again, she bought it over the phone from the East Coast.

Latham descendants preserved the story of their home in Stephenville.

M. L. and Middie Latham

Latham family photos courtesy of granddaughter Brenda Hansen

Fireplace fashioned with stone and petrified wood

North Central Region 117

The Lathams' corner lot in Stephenville gave room for a garage, an outdoor fireplace, decorative hardscaping and a surrounding wall.

The initials of stonemason C.C. Darby can be found etched in a piece of sandstone by the original kitchen door.

The Latham house, in a three-quarter view from the street corner.

The Lathams also finished their garage apartment with petrified wood.

The outdoor fireplace was designed to showcase particular stones.

A typical section of wall features the work of stonemason C.C. Darby.

Large upright logs of fossil wood stand look like statuary behind a low perimeter wall.

North Central Region 119

Rising Star : City Cannery / City Hall

According to a paragraph of text in a small history of Rising Star (Eastland County) 'copied from an old document,' a number of petrified wood 'trees were located and dug up on the Studdum Farm' southwest of the community in 1933. 'Thousands' of small rocks as well as larger trunks and limbs were uncovered and used to build the municipal building.

"Twinkle City"

City Hall Built

In 1933, under the administration of Mayor W.E. Tyler, the present handsome city hall, through the help of the CWA was erected, a picture of which is known in this edition of the Record. The city hall and adjoining building houses the water pumping plant and the fire fighting equipment as well as the offices of the City Utilities. A large part of the main building has been used for some time as a government cannery and WPA sewing room. The grounds of the city property have been improved and beautified and a small vineyard set out for practical demonstration of the growing of grapes in this section.

The city water supply is furnished by seven wells in different parts of town, furnishing sufficient water for all purposes except during severe droughts or exceptionally hot summers. At this time another well is being put down in the west part of town to add to the water supply.

A copy of a newspaper clipping, without provenance, comments on the 'handsome' city hall, built during the administration of Mayor W.E. Tyler in conjuntion with the Civil Works Administration, a depression relief agency. The text also relates that a large part of the main building had been used as a 'government cannery' and a Works Progress Administration sewing room, although local elders in Rising Star better remember it as part of the County Home Demonstration program popularized in that era.

The detailed fossil wood and stone exterior veneer of the City Hall illustrates the careful attention paid to the log-cabin-style placement of petrified wood in corners and around windows and doors.

DUBLIN : HUDSON HOUSE

The Hudson family, George W., Stella Mae, their daughter Wansyl and nephew George Allen, pose in the driveway in this photo from the 1940s.

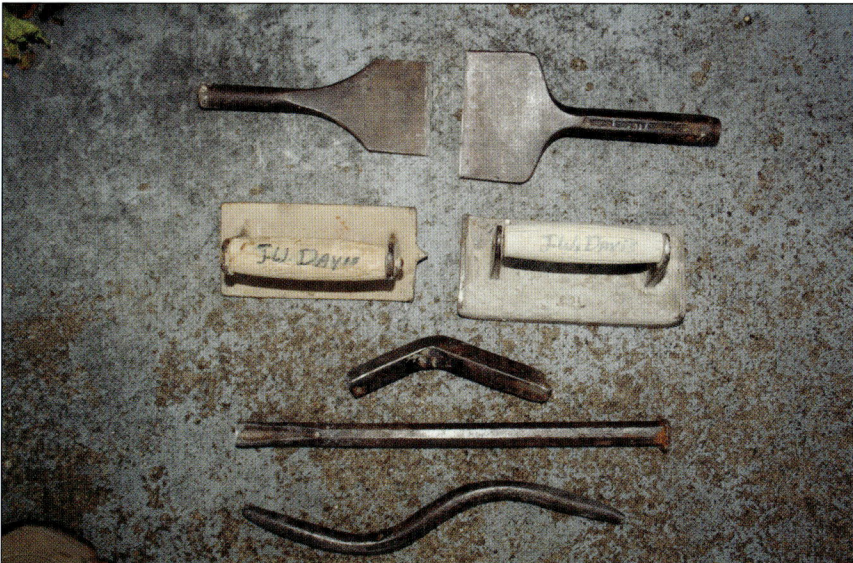

The tools of J. A. 'Rocky' Davis, the mason credited with building the Hudson House as well as others in the region.

The Hudson home outside of Dublin (Erath County), belonging to Stella Mae (Mahan) and George Washington Hudson (all the Hudson sons were named after famous men) was built by 'Rocky' Davis, a local stonemason credited with many of the rock buildings in the region.

According to the Hudsons' daughter, the fossil wood was collected mostly from nearby plowed fields but her father also went to Arkansas with a trailer to collect more rock.

The house was constructed according to a set of plans drawn by an apprentice architect who copied them from a house the Hudsons admired in Stanford. She remembers that they tore down an old house for the wood for the walls, that the foundation was as wide as a sidewalk and very deep, that the family lived in the garage apartment while the house went up and that work stopped in December of 1941 because of the war. She also remembers the hardwood floors throughout the well-built three-bedroom house, which is still in the family.

Many of the trees on the property came from Wolfe Nursery (pg. 110) in Stephenville. The pool out front was Mrs. Hudson's idea, she said, adding, "The house was daddy's, but it was mother's home."

Extensive landscaping on the grounds includes dramatic archways and concentric low walls that create a series of terraces on the sloping lot. According to the family, Mr. and Mrs. Hudson helped with some of the work on the archways.

Black and white photos courtesy of Syl Logan

Two colors of brick accent the edges of the fossil wood and stone chimney.

124 • *Stone-Tree Houses of Texas*

A view of the rear of the Hudson home

A Hudson family photograph of the backyard from a similar vantage point

The Hudson House was completed after WW II. Mr. Hudson worked for Humble Oil and collected rocks on his travels. The pecan trees came from Wolfe Nursery (pg.110).

DUBLIN : HUGHES HOUSE

Thomas Eptin and Mamie Hughes built this house on the Hico road out of Dublin (Erath County), probably in the late '30s.

According to their daughter-in-law, the property was originally a dairy farm with enough property also to raise watermelons and other vegetables, chickens and cattle; Mr. Hughes was one of the first soil conservation agents in the Dublin area. He collected the petrified wood locally as well as on the occasional trip to New Mexico and he knew where each stone came from. The house sold in 1942 for $4,000.

The couple's son, Tom Jack Hughes, helped his father with the rock, and accented a different property in Mansfield with petrified wood, creating a fish pond in the shape of the state of Texas, a water well by his garden and lining the front flower bed with the fossil wood.

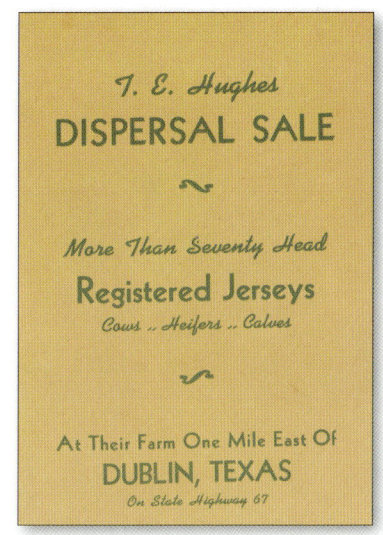

A flyer announcing the sale of Jersey cattle at 'Hughes' Hill.'

A Hughes family photo of the house and outbuildings.

Black and white photos courtesy of the Hughes family

Elaborate masonry and a variety of stone and fossil wood decorate the chimney of the Hughes home. The dramatic floral inset of the chimney is created with petrified wood and other stones, accented by quartz and crystalline formations.

North Central Region

Bronte: Youngblood House

L.T. and Alma Youngblood rocked their house in Bronte (Coke County) with stones he had solicited and received from all over the world. His documentation of the rocks – 24 single-spaced pages (and a napkin from the HiHat Lounge at the Ambassador Hotel) – records each stone and cross-references their origins -- "izing glass from Brady, Tex," "Crystal R from Brewster Co," "Small Meteor," etc.

Each identified rock is notable: "Helen Keller's birthplace," the "Home of Cortez, Old Mexico," "3 rocks from Buffalo Bill's Grave, Lookout Mountain, CO." Hundreds of donors names are noted, including Ross Wolfe, founder of the Wolfe Nursery (pg. 110) in Stephenville and A.E. Curry (pg. 140) in San Angelo.

The list includes stones from 76 Texas counties, 27 states and 25 foreign countries; in addition to stone, the masonry incorporates numerous fossils, shells, coins, ceramics, glass, arrowheads and other flint tools.

The current owners of the Youngblood House have carefully preserved this unique index.

A pattern in red brick frames the petrified wood and other unique rocks used for the chimney.

Soldier courses of brick and box-trimmed soffits frame the intricate stonework.

An entry from Mr. Youngblood's journal notes the contributions of Ross Wolfe of the Wolfe Nursery, Stephenville (pg.110). Entry #331 came from Buffalo Bill's Grave at Lookout Mountain, Colo.

Stones with their corresponding index numbers scratched into the mortar.

A logbook page lists the states and foreign countries from which stones were obtained.

Logbook and archival material courtesy of the Youngblood family

130 • *Stone-Tree Houses of Texas*

At right, numbered stones in the Youngblood home and below, the corresponding logbook page listing their type and the location where they were collected. Visible in this is number 311, collected from the White House, Washington, D.C.; number 312, 'Sapphire ore' from Montana; number 313, 'Moss Agate' from Billings, Mont.

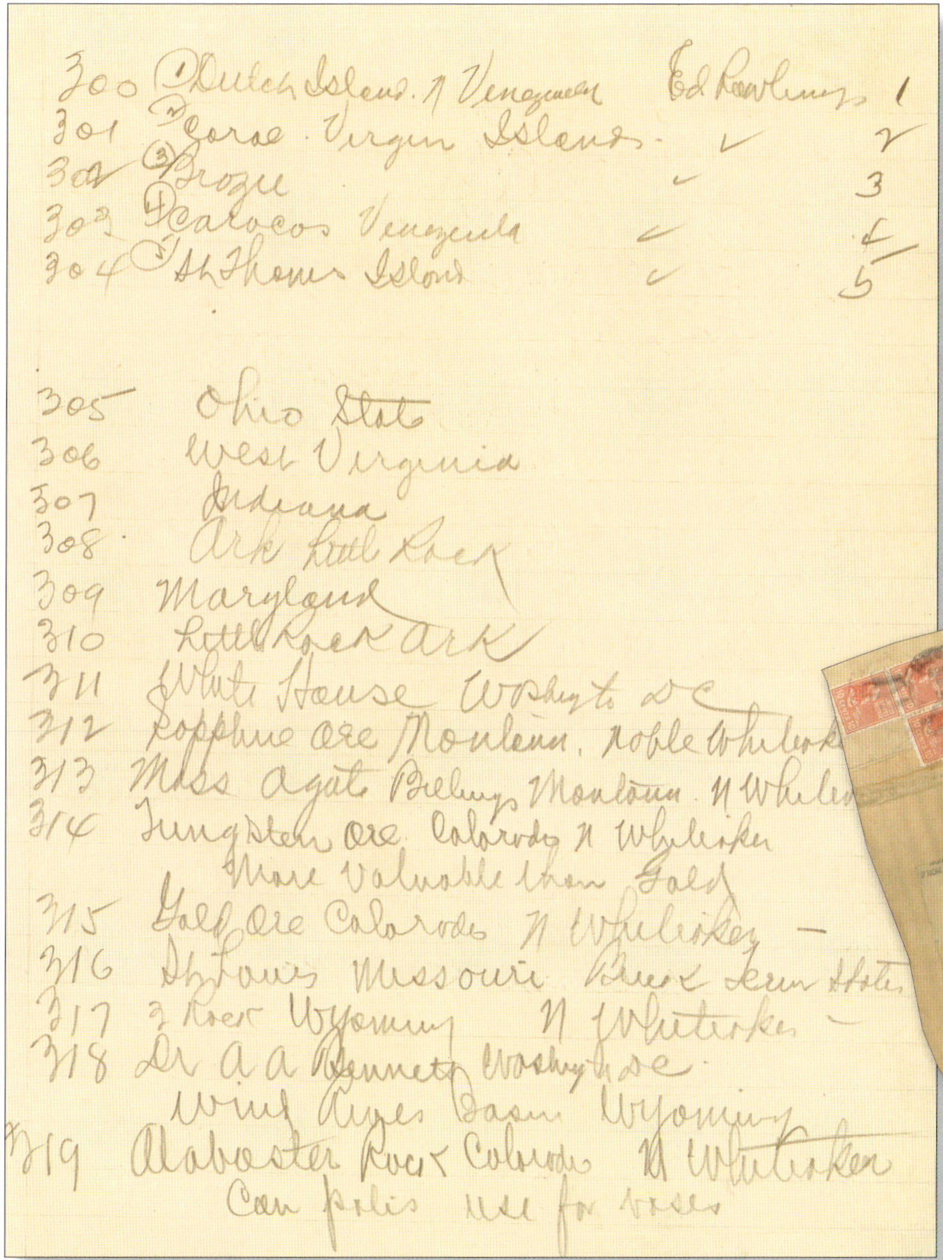

300 (1) Dutch Island N Venezuela Ed Rawlings 1
301 (2) Gorae Virgin Islands ✓ 2
302 (3) Brozil ✓ 3
303 (4) Caracas Venezuela ✓ 4
304 (5) St Thomas Island ✓ 5

305 Ohio State
306 West Virginia
307 Indiana
308 Ark Little Rock
309 Maryland
310 Little Rock Ark
311 White House Washington DC
312 Sapphire ore Montana. Noble Whitaker
313 Moss Agate Billings Montana N Whitaker
314 Tungsten ore Colorado N Whitaker
More Valuable than Gold
315 Gold ore Colorado N Whitaker —
316 St Louis Missouri Brick [illegible] State
317 [illegible] Rock Wyoming N Whitaker —
318 Dr A A Bennett Washington DC
Wind River Basin Wyoming
319 Alabaster Rock Colorado N Whitaker
Can polis use for vases

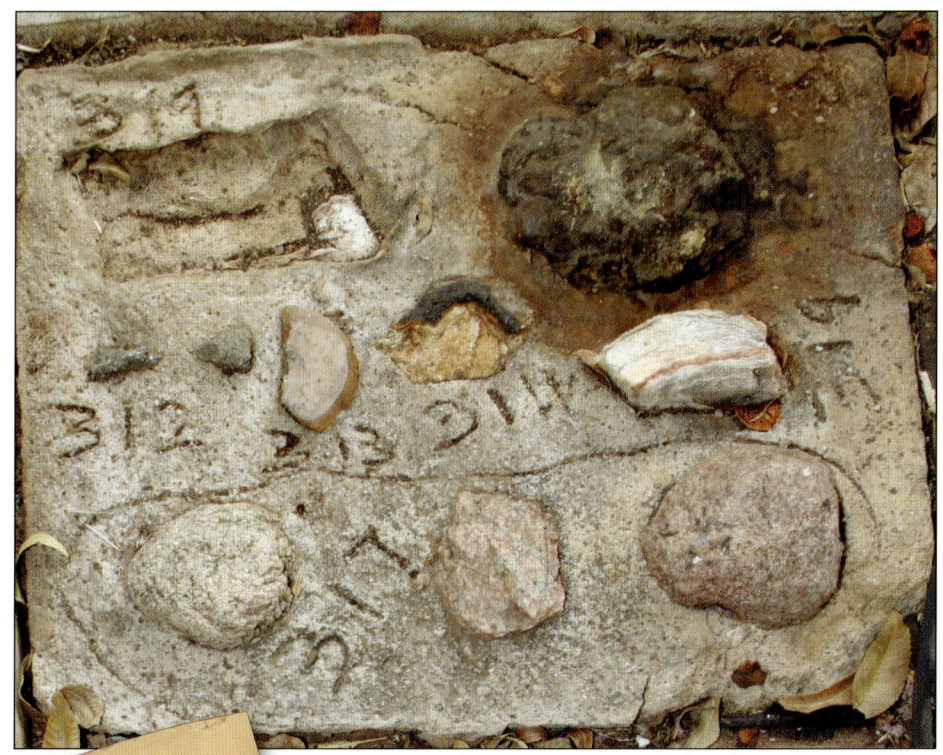

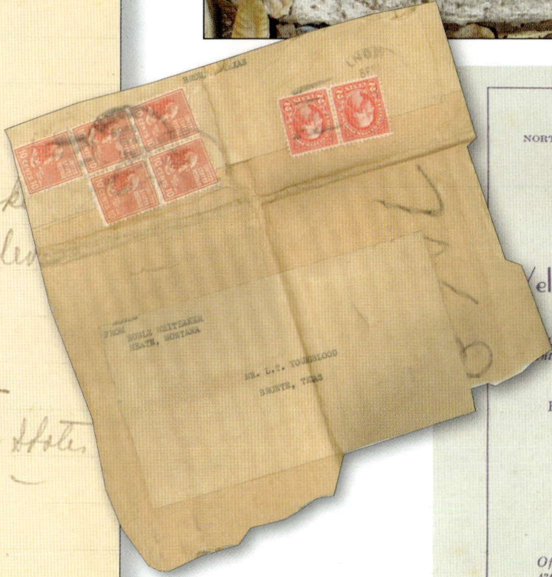

A note, brochure and mailing label from the donor of stone number 313, Mr. Noble Whittaker

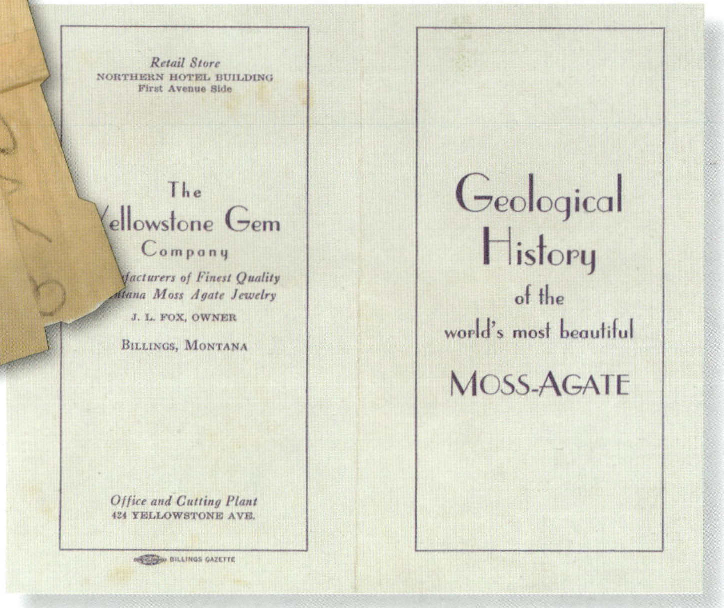

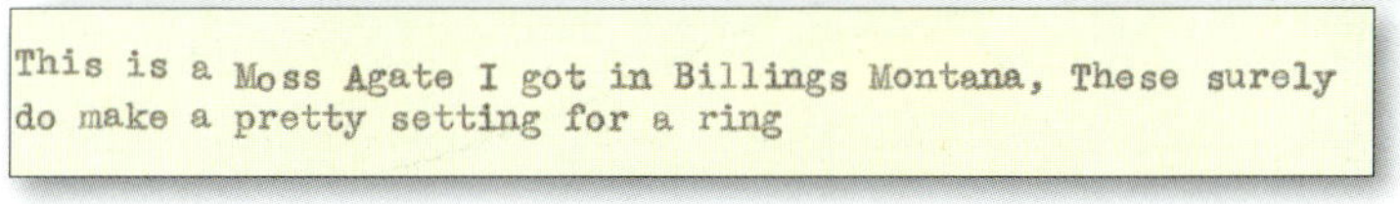

This is a Moss Agate I got in Billings Montana, These surely do make a pretty setting for a ring

San Angelo: Jennings House

The C.W. Jennings residence was constructed 1932-33 on the site of a former auto salvage yard. According to Mr. Jenning's grandson, it contains rocks from 48 of the states of the union at that time. Ollie Young's son says he remembers his dad working on this house. A striking diamond pattern suggests the Art Deco style popular in the '20s and '30s and the style is similar to others Mr. Young built.

The chimney (above left), and a stone bench from the front yard

The back side of the stone bench

A low perimeter wall featuring selenite crystals encloses the property.

Young House

Ollie Young, who had only a fourth-grade education, became an accomplished rock mason responsible for many San Angelo (Tom Green County) area homes. The former pipeline worker began laying stone during the Depression, starting out on a crew specializing in building fish ponds. Mr. Young ran his own crew throughout the 1930s, contracting with local builders to cover homes with stone. His work took him into many remote ranches and building sites often requiring him to remain on location for a week or more at a time. According to his son, he was an avid rockhound and spelunker, and always kept an eye out for interesting stone. If he noticed an area with unique rock, he would ask the landowner if he could purchase some of the material for his masonry projects.

The home shown here was Mr. Young's personal residence, built in 1935. It is a simple box-framed house with no studs; the 2 x 12-foot framing members were covered with tar paper and the rock stacked in between. The building features many unusual stones and fossils that Mr. Young acquired in his travels.

At the start of World War II, Mr. Young moved to Seattle to work in the shipyards. He passed away in 1951 and the house remains in the family today.

Mr. Young's crew work on a ranch house near Sanderson using a box-frame technique resulting in studless walls. With this method, the scaffolding rises with the building as rock is stacked directly between framing members.

Black and white photos courtesy of the Young family

The chimney of the Ollie Young House contains an architectural niche.

Ollie Young Stonemason

In black and white, a geometric design emerges from the brilliant colors of the masonry at the Ollie Young House.

Ollie Young and his sons display catfish that fed the family encampment. In remote areas, the Young family might live for a week at a time in temporary housing such as the tarpaper shack at right. His son, Jake, recounts this shack had a single-burner hotplate for a stove and an 'ice box' consisting of a hole in the ground that would be filled with ice and covered with tarps. Almost every morning the 'ice box' could be found to contain a couple of rattlesnakes.

Other examples of Ollie Young's skilled stonework include homes built for Roscoe Graham (above) and for G.B. Estes (below).

Leddy House

The San Angelo home of renowned Texas boot and saddle maker M. L. Leddy and his wife Mabel Beatrice (Williams) was built in 1936 by stonemason Ollie Young. Mr. Leddy operated a facility alongside the home that produced shoes, boots, and shirts for the military. The house was veneered with sandstone interspersed with fossil woods, granites and other unusual stones framed with brick; a rocked-in stock tank/swimming pool was an additional feature on the property. The stones for the walls had been brought in, some by rail, from "south"– ranches around San Saba, Menard, Brady and San Antonio. According to the family, the house was "built solid," over 2 x 6-inch studs with tongue and groove wood inside. The boot over the front porch was created with a wooden form and hand-cut stones inlaid into the gable end to advertise Mr. Leddy's boot business. When the house was slated for demolition some years ago, the porch was dismantled and reassembled inside Leddy's boot store downtown.

Ricci Allen, left, and Steve Eustis, right, pose with the trademark Leddy boot safely on the ground. The mosaic was removed during demolition of the original home and preserved for posterity.

Family photographs courtesy of granddaughter Beverly Allen

Northeastern Region

About the Geology

Northeast Texas consists of upper Cretaceous limestones on the western and northern margins and grades evenly to the east and southeast into Paleocene and then early and mid-Eocene sands, silts, and clays associated with the gradual filling of the Gulf of Mexico by debris eroded from the uplifted Rocky Mountains to the west and northwest.

Flanking the border with Louisiana is an uplifted area known as the Sabine Uplift where early Eocene sediments are once again exposed (Spearing, 1991).

The late Paleocene to early Eocene Wilcox Group (~55 m.y.), consisting of the Hooper, Simsboro, and Calvert Bluff Formations (Barnes, 1992), were deposited in a series of prograding deltas along the Texas and western Louisiana coasts (Xue and Galloway, 1995).

The updip portion of the Calvert Bluff deltas outcrop across southeast and east Texas. These deltaic systems typically consists of fluvial and floodplain facies, which contain terrigenous plant and animal fossil material.

In the lignite coal seams and elsewhere in the floodplain facies of the Calvert Bluff are abundant fossilized logs. Preservation of these fossil logs is typically poor, leading to large holes or cavities that often times are filled with microcrystalline quartz or sometimes smoky quartz crystals. The latter make attractive specimens for collecting.

In coal seams that are mined for electricity generation plants, large silicified (and lignitized) logs are often encased within the lignite seams and must be removed with earth moving equipment because they will not burn.

Silicified logs found in the lignites are monotypic, meaning that they consist of only one species. It is a conifer in the Taxodiaceae family, which is a family that includes Swamp (or Bald) Cypress. The fossil species somewhat resemble the modern day variety; although they did inhabit about the same environment, they are actually a completely different (and extinct) species, even.

The adjacent floodplain facies consists of these same conifers as well as a diverse assemblage of tropical, wetland hardwoods. Altogether, this defines a warm environment that had high rainfall and abundant runoff that built large deltas within extensive floodplains and swamps.

Occasionally, fossil wood also occurs in another younger formation, called the Sparta Sand (mid-Eocene, ~43 m.y.). This is a terrigenous sand (between two marine shale formations) that is cross-bedded, indicating fluvial deposition. Where found, fossil woods from this formation are similar to the next youngest terrigenous formation (Yegua Formation, described in context with the Southeast Region).

Both of the petrified wood houses in the Northeast Region occur in areas where the Sparta Sand is exposed at the surface (Barnes, 1992). However, abundant Wilcox Group fossil woods are in relatively close proximity and could also be used for construction.

— Scott Singleton

TYLER : SMITH HOUSE

Little is known about this distinctive stone-tree house in Tyler (Smith County) or who built it. The structure is one of the finest examples of the form and one of the few built with no wooden framework and solid rock and fossil wood walls. The house is located in the Azalea Historic District; it appears on a 1938 Sanborn Map and the 1940 Tyler City Directory lists the owners as Frank and Julia Smith, who are also listed as owning Economy Grocery & Market in the 1942 directory.

The interior niche encloses crystalline slabs, while the exterior holds seashells, starfish, and rock specimens.

Northeastern Region 149

Rusk: Schochler House

Laura Schochler

The Schochler House in the East Texas town of Rusk (Henderson County) remains today in the care of its original family.

The house with a stone-tree window box and a swag flourish on the porch was a wedding gift to Harmon Schochler and his bride Laura from her parents in 1933. They also received a new car.

The petrified wood used was said to come from west of Fairfield. The chimney on this home is the only one with a trunk and branch motif not located in the Caprock region.

Family photos courtesy of Max Schochler

A branch design of fossil wood is found in the chimney.

An old family photo of the Schochler Home

A window box is made completely of smaller peices of fossilized wood.

Northeastern Region 151

SOUTH CENTRAL REGION

About the Geology

The South Central Region consists of three topographic terrains: the Hill Country in the east, the Llano Uplift in the northeast, and the Edwards Plateau in the remainder.

The Hill Country and Edwards Plateau are made up of thick sequences of Cretaceous limestones, while the Llano Uplift reveals a ring of Paleozoic sediments around Precambrian igneous and metamorphic rocks uplifted in the Ouachita Orogeny (Spearing, 1991).

None of these terrains is an environment where we would expect fossil wood to exist, and for the most part it doesn't.

However, in one particular layer within the Segovia Formation of the early Cretaceous Edwards Group (106-100 m.y.) there exists a layer called the Orr Ranch Bed (Rose, 1972).

Wherever this layer is exposed (which is typically in the central portion of the South Central Region), petrified wood can usually be found in the vicinity.

The fossil wood is encased in chert nodules within a limestone matrix, which is how it became preserved in this high-energy depositional environment (the wood is sometimes found in association with Rudist shell fragments apparently built into bioherms by wave action).

It is theorized that this layer represents an unusual anoxic event within an overall oxygenated environment.

In some localities (such as the Bateman Ranch) the fossil wood trunks are bored by a marine bivalve known as the Teredo worm, or shipworm (family Teredinidae)**, further indicating these logs were washed out to sea, probably within a shallow lagoon, sank to the bottom and were attacked by the bivalve molluscs

However, before these destructive bivalves could finish their work, the logs were covered up and sealed within in an anaerobic environment where all biologic activity ceased.

The proto-fossils then acted as a nucleus that attracted free silica in the groundwater, which then encased the logs in a chert nodule.

This deposit of fossil logs is monotypic, meaning that it consists of only one species, a conifer known by the form genus name Cupressinoxylon. It is thought that this form genus is closely related to modern day junipers and cedars, which are members of the family Cupressaceae.

— *Scott Singleton*

The Petrified Forest Lodge was razed about 1991.

AUSTIN: PETRIFIED FOREST LODGE

John Stephen Woodard conceived one of the first motor courts in Austin (Travis County), building the Petrified Forest Lodge very close to the university by what then, in 1935, was Highway 2, or the "Georgetown Road." Using Austin architect Hugo Kuehne, he first built only five cabins, then added five more on the other side of the lot. The "wood" was brought in from the Glen Rose area (where he was born). His granddaughter remembers him pointing out the petrified wood in the gazebo on the square in Glen Rose, showing her that it was the same stone as his lodge.

He and his wife Alta June (Swank) Woodard owned and operated the 10 units for some years. There was probably a gas station on the corner with a little shopping center, which included a Fred Astaire Dance School.

Through the years, Highway 2 became U.S. 81, then Guadalupe Street. By 1950, Mr. Woodard had sold the lodge. It was renamed a tourist "court" and resold, declining from deferred maintenance through the 1980s and closing in the 1990s.

After it was razed, some of the fossil wood was used in the new construction and the rest was saved (in a Hyde Park neighbor's back yard) for some years, then used to make an entrance wall at Shipe Park; a plaque was installed recounting some of the history of this Austin landmark.

The handwriting on this image is that of Marvin (Woodard) Marsh, Mr. Woodard's oldest sister; her husband Wes Marsh built the "Honeymoon Cottage" (see pg. 108) in Glen Rose.

The 1937 postcard courtesy of Pam Woodard Tajima and Willena Woodard

An Austin landmark, the Petrified Forest Lodge was razed in the late 1990s but thanks to the Hyde Park Neighborhood Association, a good portion of the petrified wood was recycled. Some of the 'wood' was used in the construction of a new pharmacy; the rest was saved and used to build an entrance arch and a low wall around Shipe Park.

South Central Region 155

Harper: Peril Ranch House

Rear view, Peril Ranch House

The 93-year-old house was used as a hunting cabin for many years.

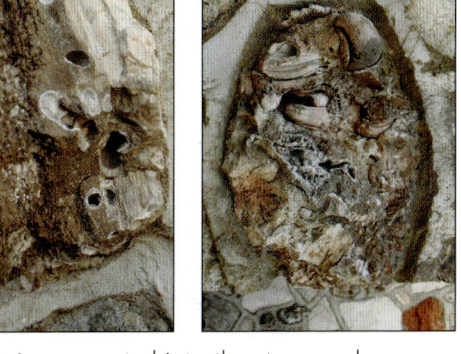

Two fossils incorporated into the stonework

Peril Nest

James A. Peril worked on the Shreiner Ranch right after the turn of the century. He was breaking horses for Mr. Shreiner when he met his future wife, Winnieola Colbath, whose dad worked for the YO, the other large ranch in the area.

In 1910, they bought a section of the Schreiner Ranch near Harper (but in Kerr County) and in 1917 built an 1,100-square-foot house using materials from a nearby outcropping of petrified wood and cretaceous fossils as well

as the prevalent limestone. When their son got married in the 1940s, they added a bedroom. The original smokehouse is now used as a guest room. They had a Delco Plant for electricity.

The Peril Ranch House is so far the oldest example of the use of petrified wood in a building in Texas. Highway 290 wasn't built until 1938.

The house more recently served as a hunting cabin but has been totally redone now, according to their granddaughter, and Peril descendants once again live there.

South Central Region

158 • *Stone-Tree Houses of Texas*

Bandera: Frontier Times Museum

J. Marvin Hunter was the "country editor" and publisher of the weekly newspaper *Bandera New Era* and the *Frontier Times*, where he recorded tales of Texas history.

According to a newspaper clipping in the Frontier Times Museum's files, Mr. Hunter began collecting frontier relics and western memorabilia in 1929; by 1932 he had run out of space and needed a building to house his fast-growing collection.

So in the midst of the Great Depression, he began to raise funds for a building by publishing paperback western-themed novels such as *The Authentic History of Sam Bass and his Gang* and offering discounted subscriptions to the *Frontier Times* as an additional enticement to his book customers. Mr. Hunter did not seek any federal funding nor "at-will" donations as he wanted the museum to remain independent of outside influence.

When enough funds had been gathered to begin construction, he hired local stonemason Hugh LeStourgeon to build a 20 x 40-foot stone structure on the site. Mr. Hunter specified that the building be made of stone for its fire resistance and that only jagged rock be used in the construction. Many of the stones came, according to Mr. Hunter, from an old rock fence built near Bandera in the late 1800s. He also reported that the use of fieldstone was new to the area and after Mr. LeStourgeon trained the local men to use it, it became very popular.

Ground was broken for the Frontier Times Museum just north of the county courthouse on Delightful Hill, Jan. 1, 1933. Construction was completed by late spring and the museum opened to the public with great fanfare on May 20.

Another clipping in the museum's files reports that the "... exterior walls are curious and odd formations of stone, stalactites and stalagmites

A picture postcard image shows the Frontier Times Museum as it appeared when it was first completed in 1933.

from caves, fossils, petrified wood, crystallized and agatized formations, vari-colored stones from over the county, and stones from historic places. Four beautiful red granite columns adorn the main entrance to the building and two more granite columns are to be added. On these columns are inscribed the names of many people who have made possible the erection of the beautiful building by subscribing to the *Frontier Times* for a record of five years."

The museum's interior walls received similar treatment and are studded with fossils and oddly shaped stones and curiosities.

The fireplace hearths are particularly detailed. The hearth in the east wall is inlaid completely with fossilized clams surrounding a large ammonite centerpiece; a millstone brought to Bandera by Mormon colonists in 1854 was placed above the arrowhead-tipped mantle. The other hearth features the name of museum founder J. Marvin Hunter spelled out in glass marbles, as well as numerous fossils, polished stone and shells, various hand tools and western memorabilia, including a muzzle-loading double-barreled shotgun, and a bullet mold mortared in "like a rock."

Within a year, the museum was full so Mr. Hunter published another book, *The Life of Big Foot Wallace*, to finance a 16 x 40-foot expansion, completed in 1934. The building was expanded again in 1935, with other minor changes being made in the years since.

After Mr. Hunter died in 1957, the museum was purchased and restored by the F. B. Doane Foundation and the collection was retained intact. In 1966, the building was recognized by the state as a Texas Historical Landmark and a plaque erected on the grounds. A second Texas Historical Marker details the contributions of John Warren Hunter, son of the museum's founder.

The property was deeded to Bandera County in 1972, but the foundation continues to administer the museum and has expanded the collections to include a gallery of western art. It is estimated that the museum's collections contain about 30,000 items, largely comprised of frontier-era relics and memorabilia but included also are such widely diverse items as shrunken heads, phonographs, hand-operated printing presses, bank safes, and a collection of 400 rare bells from all over the world. The museum is open daily and remains a popular area attraction.

Black and white photos and archival materials courtesy of Frontier Times Museum

A clipping from *The Bandera New Era* describes the 1933 opening festivities for Mr. Hunter's Frontier Times museum.

Large crowds attended the Frontier Times Museum's celebration for its 1935 expansion.

In this photo from the 1990s, the late Hugh LeSturgeon, stonemason, leans on a four-foot limestone well cap framing a window in the museum he built.

A panoramic image of the museum after several additions

The Frontier Times Museum was recognized as a Recorded Texas Historic Landmark by the state in 1966 and awarded a Texas Historical Marker medallion and descriptive plaque.

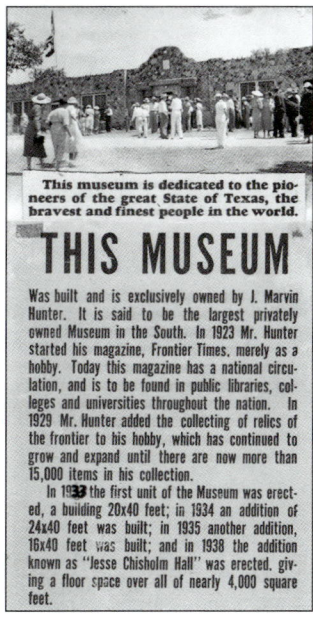

Museum promotional materials describe and document the various additions to the facility over the years.

A second Texas Historical Marker details the contributions made by John Warren Hunter, son of the museum's founder.

South Central Region

The hearth in the east wall is inlaid completely with fossilized clams surrounding a large ammonite centerpiece topped off above the arrowhead-tipped mantle with a millstone brought to Bandera by Mormon colonists in 1854.

In this interior shot of the Frontier Times Museum before the 1935 expansion, Mr. Hunter is seated in front of the east wall hearth.

A large fossil ammonite, possibly from the Pecos River, was set into the east hearth.

A fossilized coral forms a centerpiece in the 'shotgun' fireplace.

This undated image shows the museum before later expansions doubled its size.

Southeastern Region

About the Geology

The Southeastern and Southern Regions share identical geology.

The regions are dominated by the progressive infilling of the Gulf of Mexico by sediments derived from the erosion of the uplifting Rocky Mountains during the Tertiary Period (~65-2.5 m.y.).

Within this period of geologic history, the position of the coastline was determined by two primary factors: (1) the buildup of large deltas containing sediments sourced from the Rocky Mountains in New Mexico and Colorado, and (2) the eustatic sea level.

The position of the coastline determines whether there will be deposition of terrigenous fluvial, deltaic, and floodplain facies, or of marine sediments, which, in turn, determines what kind of fossils we will find in any particular formation.

Eustatic sea level (i.e. as determined by changes in either the volume of water in the world's oceans or net changes in the volume of the ocean basins) is a dominant factor in Tertiary stratigraphy because it was cyclic during much of this period, and culminated in the Pleistocene with a half dozen glacial episodes that locked up huge amounts of water and caused immense amounts of stress on all forms of life, particularly those that couldn't easily migrate (such as trees).

Because of its importance, eustatic sea level charts have been generated so that its effects can be separated from that of continental uplift / subsidence or of deltaic progradation (e.g. Haq, et al, 1987).

The Cretaceous/Tertiary boundary runs (from south to north) through San Antonio, Seguin, just east of Austin, Cameron, Corsicana, then cutting east at Greenville and continuing on to Texarkana (Barnes, 1992).

The first Tertiary terrigenous formation east and south of this boundary is the upper Paleocene and lower Eocene Wilcox Group (described in the Northeast Region chapter). Fossil wood is abundant in the Calvert Bluff Formation (described in the North Eastern Region chapter) of this group and has been used in a number of places as building material.

The houses in Hoyte and Rockdale (in the Southeast Region) and Seguin (in the South Region) are located in the Wilcox and likely used these materials to build with.

The trend continues southward, with the towns of (from north to south) Calvert, Milano, Rockdale, Bastrop, Lockhart, Luling, Seguin, and San Antonio (on the southeastern side) also located within the Wilcox Group

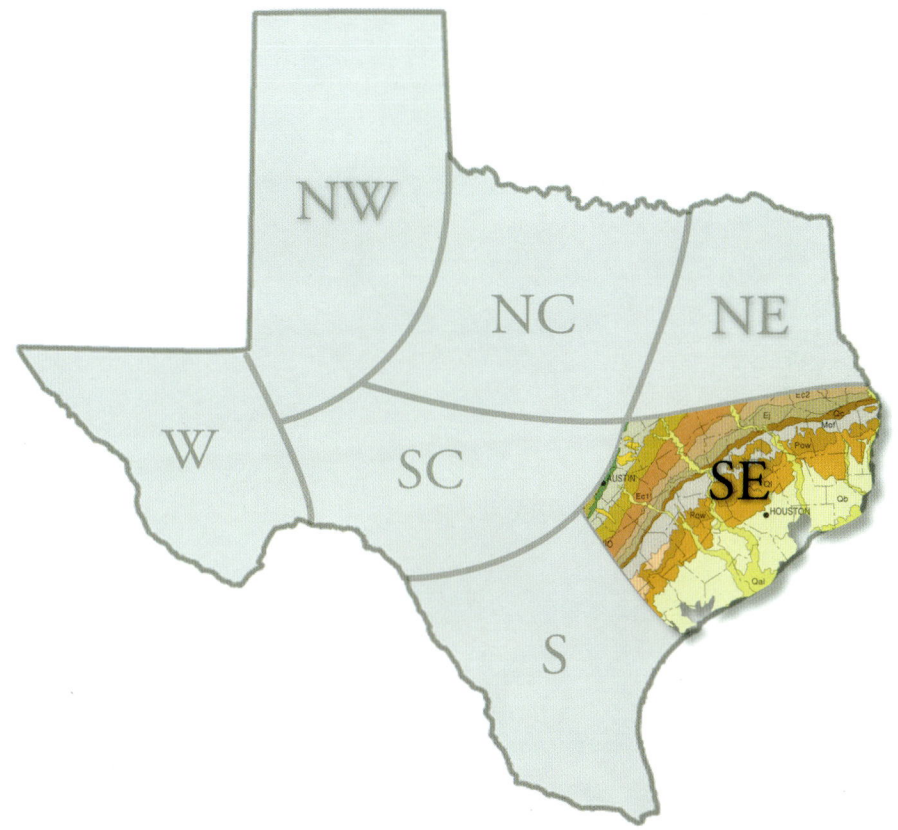

(Barnes, 1992) and having abundant supplies of fossil wood.

The next youngest fossil wood-bearing formation is the mid-Eocene Sparta Sand (~44-42 m.y.) but this is not a major wood-bearing unit because it is not thick, meaning that it is not laterally extensive. The house in Lexington is built on the Sparta Sand.

The mid-Eocene Yegua Formation (~42-41 m.y.) is thick and is a prolific wood-producing unit. The houses in Lufkin, Cooks Point, Caldwell, Snook, and Gonzales are all located within the Yegua Formation and likely used that material with which to build.

(Continued on page 235)

t E.E. Reed
n, Texas
ucted of Petrified Wood

LUFKIN: READ HOUSE

The 1935 home of E.E. "Rastus" and Emma Read in Lufkin (Angelina County) received much attention for its distinctive petrified wood exterior. The fossil wood used for the walls was collected by the Reads over a two-year period; they gathered the estimated 100 tons of fossil woods from five area counties.

The house boasted 10 rooms, including three bedrooms and two living areas. A massive piece of petrified wood, measuring 32 inches wide, 9 inches thick and 16 feet long was placed in the chimney and the house was roofed with some 19 tons of red tiles. The home was designed by architect Frank Berry, built by Jack Berry and the rock was laid by Jack Moody.

A 1988 nomination form for application to the National Register of Historic Places described the home "as an exuberant representation of the bungalow style of vernacular architecture." The home was razed in 1998.

Read family photos show their petrified-wood-covered bungalow, completed in 1935. Large logs were stacked up the chimney.

THE READ HOUSE WAS DEMOLISHED IN 1998.

Old photos courtesy of
the Read family and clippings courtesy of
The Lufkin Daily News

When the home was torn down, some of the petrified wood was recycled into this fireplace at a family hunting lodge in the Davy Crockett National Forest. This later fireplace was built to closely resemble the original.

Southeastern Region

A New House, Centuries Old, Becomes Lufkin Show Place

Reads Collected Petrified Wood For Years to Build Unusual Home

A new house, centuries old!

This describes the recently completed home of E. E. Read, located on the Houston highway just outside the city limits.

The house stands alone in Texas for uniqueness so far as can be found. Of the many transients who have stopped for an inspection of the house, none have seen its like closer than Arizona, Read said.

The material used in the construction of the house is petrified wood. This rock formation was originally logs of pine and oak wood, and required many thousands of years of burial in sand and clay to effect the conversion to stone.

So, it is gathered that while dinosaurs and various "Palaeozoic Amphibians" roamed the pine forests which, eons later would become Angelina county, the forests were also growing what ultimately became this Lufkin home.

One hundred tons of this petrified wood was used in the structure and 375 sacks of cement hold it together. This is about twice as much cement as would be used in a brick house the same size, contractors said.

The home is the result of two years work by the owners, Mr. and Mrs. Read.

Home Built of Petrified Wood

THE NEW Home of Mr. and Mrs. E. E. Read here is attracting much attention for the unusual materials that were used in construction. The Reads searched the country for two years collecting petrified wood until they had enough of the stone to build the dwelling.

The work required in this search is shown by the fact that practically every piece of the wood had to be dug from the ground. It also took a trained eye to discover the pieces that many times were barely discernible above the ground.

Farmers Joined Hunt

Read said that he would have been unable to gather enough of the material had it not been for the cooperation received by many farmers. He would spot an unusually large piece of the wood and ask the owner for it. He was never turned down on such occasions, he said.

When these large pieces were found and permission given, Read would send out a truck and men to bring them in. It usually took several hours to dig the stone from the ground and when unearthed they were quite a job to load.

One of the largest pieces in the house was given by Jim Townsend, local attorney. It was a petrified oak log, 32 inches in width, nine inches thick and 16 feet high. This was used in the chimney.

Even the mail box on the front porch is of petrified wood. Hollow on the inside and making a perfect box, this addition was sent to the Reads from Chicago by a relative.

Rocks Put In Place

It is interesting to note that as a piece was found especially adapted for a certain part of the house, it was placed into position immediately. For example two small petrified logs were placed at the front step entrance—this was the first piece of stone wood laid—and it stood some 12 months before work on the house actually started.

On "sunshiney" days, the exterior of the house fairly glistens as the rays of the sun strike the petrified rosin and sap in the wood. Every color in the rainbow can be seen on these occasions.

The cell construction of the original wood is distinct in many of the fragments of trees used in this building. The coloring is attributed to a small amount of iron which gives the beautiful red, yellow and brown tints to the "wood."

Unusual Fireplace

One of the most unique sights of the entire house is the fireplace and mantle in the living room. Each stone was carefully selected. Crevices were left for small mantle lights, a large clock and niches in which are inlaid mosaics. A horseshoe arrangement will house the clock.

That the house is really something different is shown by the number of travelers who stop for an inspection. Many of the cars drive beyond the home only to turn around and visit the unusual structure.

The house has 10 rooms—three bedrooms, two living rooms, dining room, kitchen, breakfast room and two bathrooms. It is equipped with all of the latest improvements and the interior presents as beautiful an aspect as the unique exterior.

Jack Berry was the builder, Frank Berry the architect, and Jack Moody laid the rock. All are local men and made a remarkable job of the house, Read thinks.

As an added feature, the roof of the home is of Ludowici-Celadon, a red Spanish tile composition. It weighs 38,000 pounds and blends nicely with the rest of the structure.

But the job is not yet finished. The Reads have yet to discover enough petrified wood for the double garage that is already un-

---

The new home of Mr. and Mrs. E. E. Read here is attracting much attention for the unusual articles that were used in construction. The Reads searched the country for two years collecting petrified wood until they had enough stone to build the dwelling. The home is located just outside the city limits on the Houston Highway. One of the largest pieces was given by Jim Townsend, local attorney. It was a petrified oak log 32 inches wide, nine inches thick, and 16 feet high. Jack Berry was the builder, Frank Berry was the architect, and Jack Moody laid the rock. All are local men.

"It was more or less of a dream house when we first started," Read said. "I had the idea for a number of years but it seemed an impossible job to gather enough of the wood to build a house," he added.

The wood was gathered in five counties—Trinity, Polk, Angelina, Nacogdoches and Houston. A few of the pieces came from near San Antonio where the Reads got them while on a vacation the past summer.

Read said that every spare moment during the two years was used in gathering the wood. On hunting trips he would neglect the game in search of more of the material.

The quest became so interesting that even the little son of the Reads searched diligently for the wood and often times made valuable discoveries.

Job Seemed 'Impossible'

Mrs. Read. They gathered every piece of wood used in the house, working in the late afternoons and on Sundays in their search for the precious pieces.

The Lufkin Daily News also celebrated the 'Show Place' in a story detailing the two years the Reads spent collecting and transporting the petrified wood rocks from neighboring counties. A 16-foot long, 32-inch wide log was installed in the chimney along with a selection of special stones for the mantel and fireplace. The red Spanish tile roof which covered the 10-room house. weighed about 38,000 pounds.

Thursday, October 15, 1998, Vol. 92, No. 349

Staff photos by Joel Andrews

DAVID HICKS, 21, and Mary Margaret Fenley, 4, sit on the front porch of the home their great-grandparents built in the 1500 block of First Street. The home, built in 1935 by E.E. "Rastus" and Erma Read, is in the process of being torn down. At right, Leon Huffman is dismantling the roof.

ROCKS OF AGES

Historic Lufkin home being torn down and relocated

By ZACH MAXWELL
Staff writer

It took centuries for 100 tons of petrified wood from all over Texas to form and eventually come together as a home on South First Street. In a matter of days, Lufkin's petrified rock house will be completely dismantled.

But the owners of the home, an eye-catcher for more than six decades along the busy city thoroughfare, say time will march on for the petrified wood pieces and 38,000 pounds of clay roof tiles, which will be used to build a new home on the shores of Sam Rayburn Reservoir.

"For my family, the house holds ... memories of a yard filled with beautiful rose gardens and goldfish ponds," wrote Jule Tatum Fenley, a relative of the home's owner. "When I walk around the house and think how excited my grandparents were with each rock that brought them closer to their dream, I

See ROCK HOME, Page 5A

feel connected to them."

E.E. "Rastus" and Erma Read, whose names can still be seen etched in the cement driveway with the date Oct. 19, 1935, built the home after two years of gathering large pieces of petrified wood, most unearthed from Angelina and surrounding East Texas counties.

Upon completion, *The Lufkin Daily News* ran a story on the unusual dwelling, noting that the material used was centuries old.

"While dinosaurs and various 'Palaeozoic Amphibians' roamed the pine forests which eons later would become Angelina County," the article stated, "the forests were also growing what ultimately became this Lufkin home."

Retired Dr. Royce Read is having the structure dismantled and plans to build a new home "in a more secluded spot," according to Mrs. Fenley.

"My family couldn't part with the rocks so lovingly gathered," she wrote. "My uncle has begun moving the house much the same way that it was built, rock by rock."

The home site also has petrified wood walkways and a star-shaped pond with an arch, with two large trees that have grown up precariously on top of it.

"The property was adjacent to land that my maternal great-grandfather farmed on Tulane," Mrs. Fenley stated. "My grandfather had dreamed of building this house for years."

The couple, area farmers, and relatives from as far away as Chicago sent pieces for the home. Most recently, the house was home to a Tarot card reading and fortune telling business. Many car lots and fast food establishments line the street once clustered with farm homes.

The glistening stones may leave town, but they will be nearby and they will soon be together again.

"I'm sure that my grandparents would approve," Mrs. Fenley said.

A subsequent article published in 1998 reported that the Reads' descendants were dismantling the house for relocation.

Jasper: Munson/Kinnear House

According to local history, the Callan Munson House was built in 1941 in Jasper (Jasper County). The fossil wood used in its construction was uncovered in 1938, when a bombing range was opened north of town and the military activity created craters that dislodged the wood. When Mr. Kinnear bought it, he had to go to Beaumont to find financing for the mortgage because his local bank president, who rented the house, didn't want to move and refused to make the loan.

Hoyte: Pressley House

The columns used on the front porch still show the pattern of the bark after millions of years.

THE CAMERON HERALD THURSDAY, MARCH 26, 1931

Vinyard Hill Home H. B. Pressley From Local Petrified Wood

Mr. and Mrs. H. B. Pressley who live on a fine estate called Vinyard Hill, are building a beautiful home on the site of their old home, which is near Hoyte. This will be a unique and attractive place.

Last November Mr. Pressley began the collection of petrified rocks from his vast estate and from other lands near by which will be used exclusively in the building of the home. It will be a nine room house with a basement, bath and a large Southern colonial style porch fronting East and south, 10 by 26 feet. The home will be fitted with gas pipes and plugs so that when gas comes near he will be able to get connections. There will be a Delco Light plant for immediate use. Southern chimneys will add a touch to the home. Large petrified trees will form three long columns and three half columns of rock that will complete the front of the porch. Numerous rocks have been split where the heart of the trees have formed scintillating rays in beautiful colors that will be used on the interior of the house in the construction of the mantles and book cases.

The interior of the home will be plastered and papered and woodwork will be in ivory and gray. A modern wind mill will supply the home with water from a deep well. The foundation is about completed and work on main building will be rushed and they expect to complete it for summer occupancy.

Quite a coincident is connected with the construction of the home: Roy Lane, is architect; Roy Jeter of Jeter Lumber Company is furnishing the lumber; Roy Weems is contractor for the wood work; Roy English is head of the laying of the stone; and Roy Pressley, son of the landlord, is the gallant water carrier for those employed on the building. It will indeed be a Roy-al Home.

Family photographs and clippings courtesy of Paulie Pressley McDermott and *The Cameron Herald*

This newspaper clipping from *The Cameron Herald* was kept in the family Bible.

'VINEYARD HILL'

The Pressley home, located a few miles south of Cameron (Milam County), is one of the few fossilized wood structures in Texas that is 100 percent petrified wood. According to his daughter, after he bought the property in 1908, Harold B. Pressley gathered the 65-million-year old rocks from his farmland for the next 20 years.

Designed by architect Roy Lane with a large foundation and basement to prevent settling, the three-bedroom, one-bath house was built by Roy English, a mason from Glen Rose who arrived with his trowel and stayed with the Pressley family until the house, the garage and the barn were finished. The family moved in June of 1931.

The only stone not from the Pressleys' property is an eight-foot-tall, all white "tree," used as a column for the 10 x 26-foot porch. It was a gift from a friend, hauled 10 miles from Maysfield in a Model-T truck.

The home place of the estate known as "Vineyard Hill" is still in the family. After the death of her husband Harold, Kennie Pressley lived there until she was 90 years old. Her daughter Paulie and son-in-law followed in residence and the next generation is expected to enjoy the home as well.

The Pressley House is one of the few that is 100 percent petrified wood.

A large piece of petrified wood borders the front porch at the Pressley House.

Massive stone trees serve as pillars of the front porch at Vineyard Hill.

A typical section of wall shows the 100 percent fossil wood veneer.

A curved rock to hold Mr. Pressley's pipe and matches was incorporated into the fireplace.

176 • *Stone-Tree Houses of Texas*

The barn at Vineyard Hill is faced with iron ore rock.

Mr. Pressley's initials, 'H P,' are inlaid in petrified wood above the barn doors.

The garage, later converted into an office, was also built entirely from petrified wood.

Southeastern Region

LEXINGTON: HORNUNG HOUSE

The Hornung house near Lexington (Lee County) is probably 100 percent fossil wood.

Built by the four sons of Louis and Fredericka Hornung in the summer of 1937, it is sited in the center of the 1883 Heritage Ranch. Family lore has handed down that Mrs. Hornung was not happy about having a rock house, because "in the part of Germany she was from, only poor people lived in rock houses."

Sons John, Herman, Louis Jr., and Otto began the project with a couple of rock layers from Oklahoma who, as it turned out, spent too much time in the local saloon. The sons decided they could do it themselves.

Using a flatbed truck, they loaded 65-million-year-old fossil wood from a "petrified forest" located near Dime Box, northeast of Giddings, as well as from local farmers and ranchers. Their descendants remember that the deliveries arrived almost daily. The coloration of the stones seems to be similar to "wood" found at Cooks Point. One of the porch beams was chiseled from a Winchester farmer's bull pen with a lumber wedge and sledgehammer. The foundation beam is 2½ x 3 feet thick.

The young men laid about two rows a day with no electric tools. The family remembers that a great deal of respect was given to the way the rock was found in the ground. One of the sons is quoted as saying that in the summer of 1937, they would stand and look at the different piles of rocks until they found the ones that would fit together.

The cottage-like façade belies the space inside for three bedrooms as well as a big attic and a basement; steps outside the back door led down to the cellar, which doubled as a cool guest bedroom in the summer. One of the boys designed all the rooms to open onto the dining room. All the buildings, including the two-car garage and a low wall framing the front yard, were built with the same care. Descendants are not sure why there is a longhorn designed into the chimney.

The property remains in the family.

Family photos courtesy of the Hornung descendants

This undated aerial shot from the family album shows the layout of the buildings on the Hornung place.

The Hornung brothers posed on a fence in this undated family photo.

Southeastern Region

The Hornung family is not sure why there is a longhorn design inlaid into the chimney.

A petrified stump like the one above is considered desirable by fossil collectors and rockhounds. Petrified palmwood, the state stone of Texas, can be found throughout the state, especially in the Piney Woods region.

The same style of stonework used on the house is displayed on the two-car garage.

A low fossil wood wall with arched gateways surrounds the front yard.

The expansive hearth was constructed with large logs of petrified wood.

Fossilized logs trim the garage window.

Southeastern Region

Rockdale: Copeland / Fiesler House

The Herbert and Mamie Fiesler House was completed for Rev. Copeland in 1881. The home was clad with standard wood siding until the 1950s, when Mrs. Fiesler herself spent summers collecting petrified wood and local stone in her Studebaker. The car pulled a two-wheel trailer and she employed local schoolboys to help load the materials. Farmers and ranchers helped by piling their unwanted stone along fence lines and ditches for her to pick up.

A photo of the home as it appeared originally in the late 1800s

After a remodel, but before the structure was re-configured and rocked in the 1950s

Black and white photos courtesy of Charles Caffey

Multicolored pieces of petrified wood in the chimney rise above the second story of the Copeland/Fiesler House in Rockdale.

Southeastern Region

Thousands of petrified wood pieces of different sizes and colors maximize the visual impact of the façade of the Copeland/Fiesler House.

The doghouse at the Fiesler Home is also petrified wood and is the only existing example found.

Large fossil wood logs flank both sides of the entry; at the top of each, stones have been placed in a radiating pattern around a large roundel housing a light fixture. When taken as a whole, the design is reminiscent of a candle.

Southeastern Region 187

Coffield House

Evident in the early photo of the Coffield House are a low stone fence bordering the property, a decorative well and a two-car garage.

Rockdale Chamber of Commerce

This fossil wood house in Rockdale (Milam County) now serves as offices of the Rockdale Chamber of Commerce.

It was built by H.H. "Pete" Coffield in the mid-'30s as a rental unit. According to local history, Mr. Coffield made a great deal of money in a varied career in oil and other industries, including "war surplus," and he served as a commissioner of the state prison board.

A combination of architectural features included modified buttresses, brick trim on entries and windows (including decorative round portals on the front and under one of the steep pitched gables) and a tile roof with "gingerbread" eaves. It has been assumed that the many outbuildings and landscape features around stone tree houses could be attributed to left-overs from the many stones required to find the pieces to fit together "like a jigsaw puzzle" of one of the structures.

Black and white photo courtesy of Rockdale Chamber of Commerce

Southeastern Region 189

Cooks Point: Chaloupka House

Wilton W. Chaloupka with his wife Libby moved in 1934 to Cooks Point (Burleson County). The Chaloupkas and members of the Urbanovsky family became partners in the Cooks Point store. Two years later in 1936 the Chaloupkas expanded into real estate when they purchased the estate of John Urban, eventually selling lots to as many as 25 area families.

Mr. Chaloupka completed this distinctive Cooks Point home in 1940. The home is covered almost entirely with petrified wood. Newspaper clippings of the day report he did most of the work himself, right down to the drawing of the plans.

A skilled carpenter in additon to his other interests, Wilton Chaloupka went on to build three additional houses including the Urbanovsky House (pg. 192) next door from petrified wood as well as a store and a church. The house remains in the family.

Wall sections reveal intricate arrangements of hundreds of pieces of fossil wood.

Mr. and Mrs. Chaloupka pose in front of their home.

A family snapshot of the home

A 1961 newspaper article describes the petrified wood home of Wilton Chaloupka, noting he built three additional houses and a church with the material.

The Chaloupka home underwent renovations in 2009.

Family photos courtesy of Tracy Chaloupka Wine and Patsy Albright

Southeastern Region

URBANOVSKY HOUSE

In the same block in Cooks Point near the Old San Antonio Highway, the history of three petrified wood houses intimately connect the Drgac, Urbanovsky and Chaloupka families.

The Urbanovskys and the Chaloupkas (see pg. 191) operated the Cooks Point Store together, as well as a hammer and grist mill where they processed feed to be sold at the store (which has been razed).

Active in the church, the families donated the land for the site of a new Cooks Point Brethren Church (pg. 197) and collected and contributed the petrified wood that was used to rock it. The church has also been razed; the site is now the cemetery.

Two brothers-in-law, Emil Urbanovsky and Wilton Chaloupka, built the several houses in the 1950s; they gathered the fossil wood from farmland around Tunis and Providence, hauling it back to Cooks Point in the earlier days by wagon.

According to the descendants of these families, the men would ask people if they had any petrified wood and if they could buy it. Most of the time, it was available for the digging. They eventually accumulated a "mountain of rocks," so many that there was enough for all three houses, their service station, and the church.

The family says Ernest Treeter, the mason, was "an artist"; he used iron ore rock and limestone to bring out the different colors. They dug down through the clay to put footings all around the house for the beams.

The Cooks Point Store was co-owned and operated continuously for 36 years by members of the Chaloupka and Urbanovsky families. Above, the store is pictured in 1933 without any rockwork.

The Urbanovskys' fossil-wood home was built with the assistance of Caldwell master stonemason Ernest Treeter.

This image from 1937 shows that the store has received a new façade and stone columns have been added to the uprights on both sides of the gas pumps.

In this undated image a petrified wood and stone veneer has been added to the entire building.

Family photos and clippings courtesy of Tracy Chaloupka Wine and Patsy Albright

Southeastern Region 193

Drgac House

The Drgac House was the home of Ed and Fannie Drgac.

During the 1940s and into the '50s, Wilton Chaloupka and Emil Urbanovsky, their sons-in-law, with the assistance of Caldwell master mason Ernest Treeter, rocked the Drgac House, their own homes, their Cooks Point Store and several others, as well as the Cooks Point Brethren Church.

The homes share similar details, such as multiple projecting gables and archways. The rock veneers also share stylistic similarities.

The Drgac home in bloom.

Double petrified wood archways frame a porch on the east side of the home.

A side view of the Drgac home faces the Cooks Point Brethren Church.

Southeastern Region

Countless loads of fossil wood and native rocks were hauled in from around the area to rock the three houses, their store, a church, and more.

COOKS POINT BRETHREN CHURCH

After the first church was destroyed by a severe storm in April of 1940, a decision was made to rebuild the Cooks Point Brethren Church in a new location. The farms of Vince Hyvl and Fred Paul provided the petrified wood for the structure and Wilton Chaloupka drew up the plans for the church. Both he and Emil Urbanovsky donated one acre of land in the center of Cooks Point – other members of the congregation supplied labor. The finished church was dedicated May 25, 1942, with the total cost for the building said to be around $900 including $75 for a brass bell purchased second-hand from the Caldwell public schools. The church remained there until the congregation moved into a new church across State Highway 21 in 1959, and the older church building was dismantled.

The new Cooks Point Brethern Church sign is covered in fossil wood.

The church was demolished in 1959.

Black and white photo courtesy of Patsy Albright

On the farms of Vince Hyvl and Fred Paul of Providence was a large amount of petrified wood stone. Wilton W. Chaloupka, a member of the church, had experience as a carpenter and was also experienced in work with petrified stone. He then began drawing plans for the church. Emil Urbanovsky volunteered to do the hauling, and others offered labor.

Mr. Chaloupka and Mr. Urbanovsky donated one acre of land on Highway 21 in the center of Cooks Point to the church. Both members and non-members assisted in the building. Henry Williams was the only hired hand but apparently did not work every day, since less than twenty five dollars was spent on labor. A brass bell, bought for seventy-five dollars from the Caldwell Public Schools, was placed in the steeple. In all, the building cost about $900.

This lovely church of petrified wood stone was dedicated on May 25, 1942. Sunday School classes were held in an SPJST hall next to the church. Later, a cemetery was added in the back.

Caldwell : Woodson House

Jim Woodson and his brother began Woodson Lumber in 1913 in Caldwell (Burleson County). In 1936, he had rocked his two-story house rocked with petrified wood and other local stone. It is thought many of the other building materials were leftovers from his construction jobs. Three barn doors bolted together were used for the garage door, broken scrap tiles were laid in the foyers, and no two windows are the same size. The house included four bedrooms, an attic, a basement and – exceptional for the decade – four bathrooms. The rockwork is attributed to stonemason E.K. Treeter, who is credited with many other homes in the area.

E.K. Treeter — Stonemason

Master stonemason Ernest K. Treeter (1910-1965) of Caldwell built or contributed to many of the stone-tree buildings in the Brazos Valley during the 1930s and '40s – in Cooks Point, Bryan, Somerville, Caldwell, and Snook; one of his best is the Kerr House (pg. 216) in Columbus.

Born in Germany to a brick mason father, he was already a master mason when he came to Texas at 16 years old in 1926; both immigrated to America as Hitler was coming to power.

Throughout his working years, E.K. Treeter advised and helped many home owners in building their own houses and was well known for the artistry of his work.

Examples of Ernest Treeter's stonework include the Caldwell homes of Richard Bowers (below) and Melvin Deutsch (right).

Treeter and crew.

Burleson County Fairgrounds Ticket Office

Treeter and his crew apply the fossil wood pieces on the ticket office of the Burleson County Fairgrounds.

Front view ticket office Burleson County Fair Grounds

Master mason E. K Treeter rocked the Burleson County Fairgrounds ticket office. It was a National Youth Administration project and the first of numerous commissions of LaVere Brooks, a young architect from Somerville.

LaVERE BROOKS

I was born in Somerville the year of the Armistice, and grew up the youngest of seven children during the depression years. After finishing Somerville High School I attended the Art Institute of Chicago for one year, and then enrolled in the Department of Architecture at Texas A&M. I graduated on Friday night, May 13, 1942, and went into the army the next day as a "brass lieutenant". While a sophomore at A&M I was asked to do the first building I ever designed, it was the ticket office for the Burleson County fair grounds. I am enclosing a picture of this. To my knowledge the building is still there. Since that time, I suppose I have been the Architect for over a $100,000,000.00 worth of projects around the United States, but the first building an Architect does is always the one I will never forget. — LaVere Brooks

This paragraph about young architect LeVere Brooks was found in the *Burleson County History*. The ticket office was the first building he designed.

Black and white photos courtesy of Johnny Treeter and the Burleson County Library

Southeastern Region 201

Snook: Elsik House

Willie T. and Isabel (Macek) Elsik bought a small farm house in the early 1930 outside of Snook (Burleson County) and began to cover it with fossil wood and stone. The Elsiks and family members spent the next several decades expanding and rocking the house.

Much of the material used was gathered from around the property and a nearby gravel pit and also from Big Bend and other collecting areas. Mr. Elsik was a rockhound and a lapidary artist. Family friend Caldwell stonemason E.K. Treeter helped with the rock work.

Three generations of Elsiks have resided in the home and it remains in the family today.

Mr. Elsik and his children on the porch of the original home. The other two black and white photos show the Elsik home undergoing expansion and receiving its stone exterior. The garage at the right contained lapidary equipment and a workshop.

Black and white photos courtesy of the Elsik family

Southeastern Region

Somerville: Nedbalek House

A winch truck was used to load the largest pieces of petrified wood for the Nedbalek House in Somerville (Burleson County). The home was built with wood from the Snook area by William 'Bill' Nedbalek, perhaps with assistance from E.K. Treeter, in the early 1940s.

Black and white photo courtesy of Craig and Keith Connor
Color photos by Shari Lane-Davis

L.C. Hudson House

The Hudson House in Somerville (Burleson County) was built in 1950. The Hudsons did much of the work themselves, including digging the foundation by hand three feet down to clay, as well as acquiring the petrified wood from area farms. Master mason E.K. Treeter was hired to lay the rock incorporating the fossil wood as well as red "iron ore stone" and native limestone. Family members who observed Mr. Treeter at work on the home call him an "artist" and say that he laid out the stones on the ground and selected each one individually by color and size for maximum effect. When the home was finished the Hudsons sold the left over petrified wood, the quantity being found sufficient to completely cover two additional homes.

The straight lines and smooth surfaces distinguish the pillars of the Hudsons' entry.

Unusual fossil specimens highlight the walls of the L.C. Hudson House.

Family photos show their house from all sides.

Photos courtesy of the Hudson family

Stone-Tree Houses of Texas

Choice pieces of fossil wood decorate the Hudsons' fireplace hearth.

A fossilzed cycad, a plant common in the Jurassic, was laid in the chimney.

Intricate stonemasonry typifies the work of master stonemason Ernest Treeter.

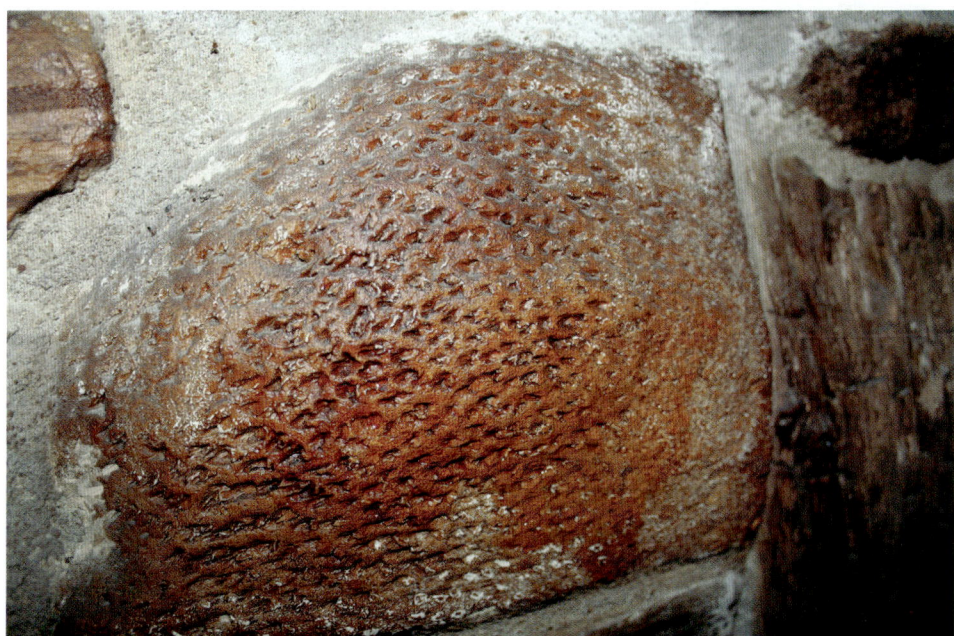
The masons mortared in special stones throughout the fireplace.

Brenham: Meyer House

This three-bedroom, one-bath house was built in 1937 for Walter and Maria Ann Meyer in Brenham (Washington County) by stonemasons Benjamin and Carl Whitmarsh (see pg. 212). The project included a garage, which was built the year before the house, and a small potting shed. The property is still in the family.

In addition to stone and petrified wood, cultural artifacts such as jugs, bottles and toys, enliven the walls of the building.

A repaired area in the rear of the wall damaged in a salt dome explosion doesn't quite match the surrounding stone work and illustrates the difficulty in duplicating the artistry of original stonemasons, the Whitmarshes.

A window box features, among other objects, screws, a horseshoe, a toy motorcycle and a doll figurine.

Southeastern Region

Benjamin Whitmarsh  Stonemason

Benjamin Whitmarsh (1891-1951) was a Washington County master stonemason who, with his son Carl (1914-1989), worked on many of the rock buildings in Brenham and the surrounding areas during the 1930s.

According to a daughter-in-law, the Whitmarshes rocked the cannery, the library, the American Legion Hall, the Lutheran Church, the Meyer House (pg. 210), and many others in Brenham using petrified wood from a large concentration near Lake Somerville and other local deposits. His work often took him out of state and even to Mexico. In later years, Carl became a well-known mason in his own right. He also did the masonry work on the Zboril House (pg. 228) in Garwood.

At left, a miniature memorial created with petrified wood placed in tribute to Ben Whitmarsh at his grave in Brenham by George Engelbretson of Bryan.

At right, three examples of residences rocked by a Whitmarsh share a stylisitc similarity; below, Carl Whitmarsh's garage; facing page, Brenham American Legion Hall, a WPA project.

212 • *Stone-Tree Houses of Texas*

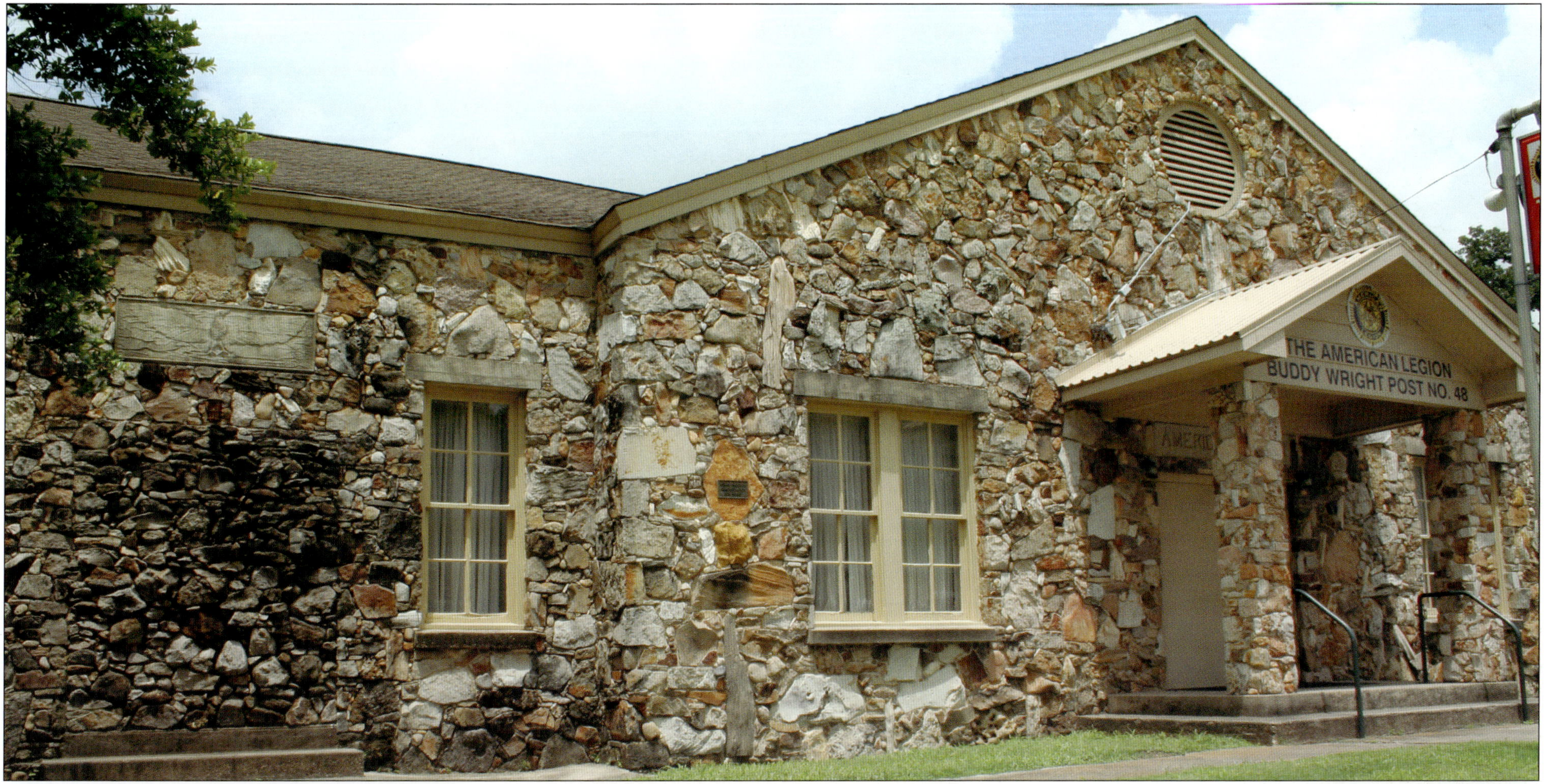
THE AMERICAN LEGION
BUDDY WRIGHT POST NO. 48

WORKS PROGRESS
ADMINISTRATION
1935 — 1937

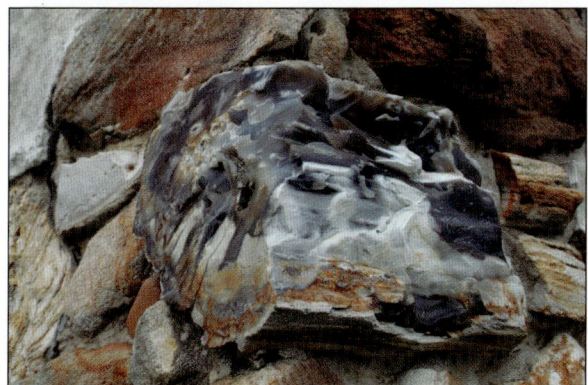

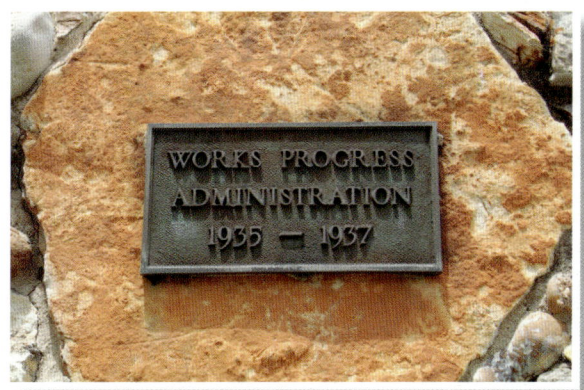

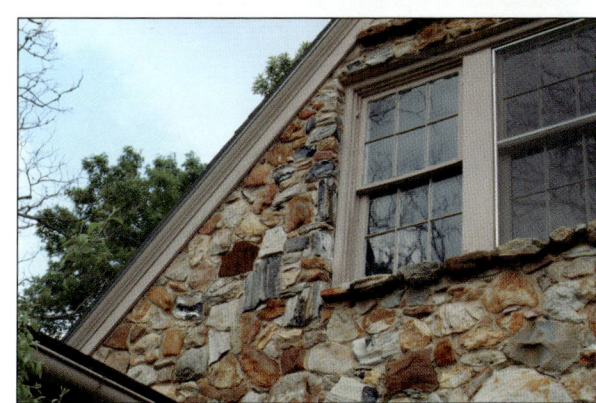

The Public Cannery in Brenham was a Depression-era project of the Works Progress Administration. The masons were Benjamin Whitmarsh and his son Carl. They collected the petrified wood and the other rocks from a creek north of Brenham. There are two outhouses built with petrified wood in the back.

Brenham : Public Cannery

The Public Cannery in Brenham (Washington County) was built as a Works Progress Administration project in 1938. Local farmers brought their produce to the facility for processing by the county, which kept half as payment. Later, the building was used as a jail for some years and in 2004 it was listed in the National Register as part of the Brenham Dowtown Historic District. It now awaits renovation.

Two sections of the cannery building demonstrate the skill of mason Benjamin Whitmarsh.

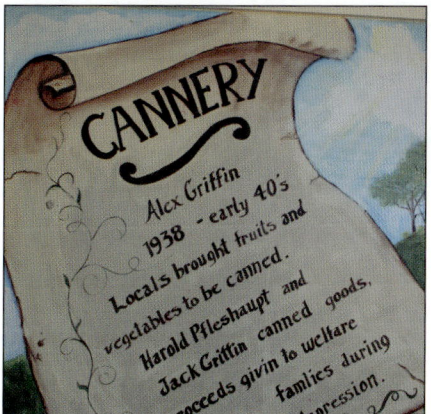

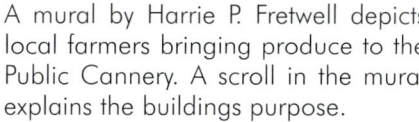

A mural by Harrie P. Fretwell depicts local farmers bringing produce to the Public Cannery. A scroll in the mural explains the buildings purpose.

One of the large steam vessels used in the canning process

Black and white photo courtesy of National Register of Historic Places

Southeastern Region 215

Columbus: Kerr House

'Fort Kerr'

Ralph and Margaret Cooper (Cole) Kerr started building their house by the river in Columbus (Colorado County) in 1947. They had sold their house in Houston (because Mr. Kerr was convinced that there would be a nuclear attack there) and moved to Hearne. The summer of 1949, they moved into the new house – before it was completed; a Kerr daughter remembers that neither the roof nor the windows were finished and that they sort of "camped out" that summer with pieces of tin over the openings to keep out the rain. She believes that they gathered the rock from more than one place, but that a lot of it was purchased from around the Caldwell area.

"It was a group effort," she remembers – "Dad supervised." She and the other children helped gather stones of just the right size to fit in where they were needed.

Master stonemason Ernest Treeter came over from Caldwell and got the building started. He taught the sons to lay rock, helped build the wooden forms for the windows and came back later to help finish the chimneys, where he and Alan Kerr left their signatures in the mortar in 1949.

The house is rocked almost completely with petrified wood. Although not 100 percent fossil wood, this house is an outstanding example of its use because of the quality of the large pieces of petrified wood incorporated into the walls and the two chimneys.

'Fort Kerr' has two chimneys and is rocked almost completely with petrified wood.

Situated on a high bank above the Colorado River, the distinctive Kerr residence, which the family called 'Fort Kerr,' was completed in 1949 after two years of labor by Mr. Kerr and his sons working in conjunction with Caldwell stonemason E.K. Treeter.

The unique long, low profile of the Kerr House

Gnarled petrified wood logs were fitted on corners, the petrified knothole laid horizontally.

218 • *Stone-Tree Houses of Texas*

An entire wall of petrified wood forms the hearth for the front fireplace in the Kerr House; the second fireplace is brick on the inside.

An inscription in the mortar on the back of the front chimney reads: 'E.K. Treeter Caldwell Tex. Nov. 1, 1944.' Mason Treeter helped the Kerr family construct their home.

The front chimney, exterior view

Gonzales: Halamicek House

The Halamicek house at Gonzales (Gonzales County) was built in 1932 of stone and fossil woods collected from "all over the country" by Mr. and Mrs. E. F. Halamicek. Designed by local architect Rudolph Nagel, construction took a master brick mason from San Antonio about two years to complete. According to newspaper reporter Jack Ball, "No expense was spared …"

A full basement of reinforced concrete with heavy cross timbers and 4 x 6-inch beams support the main structure. The concrete and stone exterior walls are 26 inches thick in places. Each stone was carefully cleaned, stacked and classified before being laid by the master stone mason. The article also stated that the doors, moldings, hinges and other hardware were custom made in San Antonio, that the floors were hardwood and many features were "tailored into the walls."

The spacious home features four bedrooms and 'an exceptionally large tub and shower' upstairs, with a large kitchen and breakfast nook, dining room, and living room downstairs. French doors lead to a sun room and a patio. The fireplace is quartz.

Large and small pieces of inlaid petrified wood enhance the arched entry around a solid oak door; one of seven exterior doors.

A 1988 clipping of an article by Jack Bell from the Gonzalez County Archives describes the Halamicek home in detail.

Photo and unattributed clipping courtesy of the Halamicek family

Newspaper clipping text

by: Jack Ball

Built in the mid-thirties, constructed of hard stones from all over the United States and Canada, and an ageless charm and beauty that fits any era…that's the home of the Mrs. E. F. Halamicek estate located on St. Joseph Street.

Mr. Rudolph Nagel of Gonzales was the architect of this most unusual home, and still recalls in detail the attention and loving care which went into its construction. No expense was spared by Mr. Halamicek, including the initial intention of placing gold fixtures in the bath rooms. This feature was abandoned after the fixtures arrived and did not live up to his expectations.

Doors, moldings, hardware, plaster over metal lathe. Obviously nothing has been done to them since the original construction. Yet, one has to look close to find the few hairline cracks at the corners of a few doors or windows.

There are four bedrooms and one bath upstairs…and hardly a square corner in the whole house. Arches and ovals abound. The upstairs walls were originally done with exquisite wall paper. All floors are hardwood. Almost every inch of usable space has been utilized, with many built-in dressers and mirrors actually tailored into the walls.

The downstairs consists of a large kitchen and breakfast nook, beautiful arched dining room, living room hinges, etc. were custom made in San Antonio. Each stone was individually selected, cleaned, classified, and stacked before installation by a master brick mason from San Antonio. It's been said that Mr. Jim Rodriguez, as a boy, helped with cleaning the stones. It took about two years to complete the construction.

The home has a full basement, with reinforced concrete walls around the entire perimeter of the structure. Cross members supporting the main structure consist of four by eight inch supports, I-beams, and a variety of other heavy cross members. One has to see this fascinating old home in order to really understand and appreciate the workmanship and materials which went into it.

Although almost fifty years old, the home is still in an excellent state of repair. Exterior walls are more than a foot thick, and all downstairs walls were originally done with extra-thick with a most unusual quartz fire place, solid oak front door, customized french doors leading to a sun room with lovely mosaic tile on the floor, hallway and wide staircase, large bedroom and a big full bath with an exceptionally large tub and shower.

A total of seven doors lead to the outside areas, patio, and car port. The full basement has a full concrete floor, with the exception of an eight by ten foot dirt area in the southeast corner. This, apparently, was the root cellar.

The exterior is a myriad of hard stones, gathered by Mr. and Mrs. Halamicek from all over the country. They include a number of petrified woods and an old grinding wheel. The grinding wheel was found by Mr. Fred Halamicek in Canoe Creek near Ottine Community. The roof is constructed of asbestos slate, a truly lifetime material.

This is indeed a structure of fascination, timelessness and endurance.

Southeastern Region

Houston: Helweg House

Although she doesn't recall exactly when the construction started on their lot in Houston, what Beatrice Helweg remembers is that in 1948, she brought her new baby daughter home from the hospital to the new house her husband Elo had built using petrified wood. His helpers included his carpenter brother Bernard who lived next door and his stonemason father-in-law Adolph Kramer from Brenham. The Helweg family lived there until their daughter was in high school. She says her husband "had a thing for petrified wood."

They gathered the rocks from around Somerville, from around her grandfather's farm; another of Elo's brothers came from Dickenson with his big truck to carry them. She says that her father would spend the week in Houston working on their house and go back to Brenham on the weekends. Elo worked for a steel company, so they used steel they welded themselves as forms for the arches.

The house still stands, small and unique but so far preserved in the midst of the larger homes surrounding it.

Family photos of Helwegs enjoying the snow.

Adolph Kramer, father-in-law of Elo Helweg and stonemason from the Brenham area

Family photos courtesy of Beatrice Helweg

Southeastern Region

The Eve's Garden complex includes a main house, and several outbuildings including a two-story garage apartment. The property is operated today as an event facility.

224 • *Stone-Tree Houses of Texas*

Brookshire: Longenbaugh House / Eve's Garden

George Longenbaugh is remembered as 'a really fun guy.'

George Longenbaugh moved to Texas from his native Louisiana. He was a successful rice farmer with over 200 acres under cultivation, he loved rocks, and he shared this stone-tree house in Brookshire (Waller County) with his wife Eva Belle.

When the big rice trucks were not being used to haul rice, he and his friend Rufus England (pg. 226) drove them out to West Texas, New Mexico, Colorado and beyond to collect rocks for the house of his dreams. He designed it, drew up the plans and started construction in the early 1940s. Petrified wood was used in all the buildings – the house, the three-car, two-story garage with an apartment above, the well house and the summer kitchen. Allen Glueck was the mason.

Today the buildings and landsacping have been revived and renewed. The complex, Eve's Gardens, can now host weddings, retreats and other special events.

**Family photo courtesy of
the Brookshire Public Library and Anice Divin**

The first building constructed was the outdoor summer kitchen (since re-purposed as a guesthouse). It included a large indoor hearth, custom plumbing and fixtures intended for preparing wild game.

Stonemason Allen Glueck built the fireplace in the main house from hundreds of pieces of stone and fossil wood. In the mantel, quartz crystals are interspersed between the vertical pieces of petrified wood.

Southeastern Region

England House

According to the current owner, the England House was built in 1949 by Rufus England in Brookshire (Waller County). Three different blueprints were drawn up by architect F. Perry Johnston, calling for the latest and best of everything, including aluminum windows which were unusual for the time, a porte cochere and a slate roof (which lasted almost 50 years). One of the rejected blueprints called for cedar shakes on the walls, not petrified wood. The house originally had three bedrooms; a storage room was added on in the 1970s with the extra stone left over.

The stone came from all parts of Texas; they selected pink granite from Marble Falls, some sandstone from West Texas, some from Madisonville.

The current owners were told that the mason was a very artistic German man and that he laid the stone out on the ground first to determine the placement of the rocks. Little stone shelves are mortared into the porch wall and there are designs in the walls.

Rufus England and George Longenbaugh (pg. 225) were good friends.

The hearth incorporates Mr. England's rock collection, including an arrowhead.

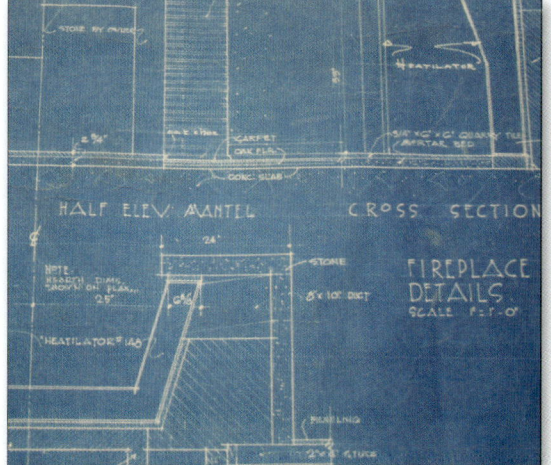

The current owners preserved the 1948 blueprint by Houston architect F. Perry Johnston.

Blueprint courtesy of Nancy Denmark

Southeastern Region

Garwood: Zboril House

Construction began on William and Viola Zboril's home in Garwood (Colorado County) just before World War II but the house remained unfinished (wrapped in black tar paper) until stonemason Carl Whitmarsh (pg. 212) of Caldwell returned from overseas to complete the work. Mrs. Zboril says that most of the fossil wood was gathered from the area around Caldwell, where farmers were paying to have it removed from their fields. When this proved too time-consuming, the family purchased wood from others willing to gather it.

Fossil wood from Caldwell and limestone from Lamesa cover the Zboril house.

Fossil wood logs form the letter 'Z' on a detached garage added later.

Petrified wood logs project end-on over the door and frame the entryway alcove.

Southeastern Region 229

HUNTSVILLE : WILLHOITE HOUSE

In the summer of 1938, Oto A. Willhoite hired his brother Paul as contractor and began construction of a large fossil wood and stone home in Huntsville (Walker County). Oto and his wife Edith had seen a rock house in Austin that they admired, secured the plans, and after a few modifications had it built on their lot in Huntsville.

The stonemason hired for the job was W.H. Archer and family members recall that the family took Mr. Archer "somewhere in West Texas" to select the rock used. The uncut stone and petrified wood were then carefully fitted together in jigsaw puzzle fashion. No wood was used in the construction of the walls – they are solid stone and up to a foot thick in places.

Distinctive features of the house include a steeply pitched roof line, arched doorways, stone window boxes and fossil wood window ledges.

The Willhoites occupied the residence until 1945 when they moved to Austin. There, they purchased the house that served originally as the inspiration for their Huntsville residence. That house was removed to make way for Loop 1 (Mopac).

The home has been recognized many times over the years. The Huntsville Texas Historical Resource Survey called it "certainly the most outstanding masonry revival-styled dwelling in Huntsville." In 1988, it was featured in Huntville's Second Annual Christmas Homes Tour and its story has been told several times in local newspapers.

The stone trees for the Willhoite House came from 'somewhere in West Texas.'

A 'rockhound mix' of stones went into this window box.

The Willhoites used stones they had collected on vacation for the fireplace hearth, including granite, fools gold, an arrowhead and an Apache tear.

Southeastern Region

THE HUNTSVILLE ITEM

Thursday, March 11, 1999 — Vol. 150—No. 70 — http://www.itemonline.com — 50 CENTS

Historic Houses: The Willhoite House

Gaineses have blended new with unique old

Editor's note: This is the first in a series of stories by The Huntsville Item covering some of the historic homes and buidings in our area.

By Michael Ann Straughan
The Huntsville Item

Hidden behind the oldest and largest magnolia trees in town is the Willhoite House, a two-story rock house with Tudor Revival stylistic features owned by Lewis and Ila Gaines.

This 1938 house sits on an acre of land where 13th Street dead-ends into Avenue P.

It has been featured in the City of Huntsville-commissioned "Historic Resources Survey of Huntsville, Texas" by Hardy-Heck-Moore, cultural resources management consultants from Austin, and Dan Utley, a historian from Austin. Here, the Willhoite House was referred to as "certainly the most outstanding masonry, revival-styled dwelling in Huntsville. Intricately crafted brick and stone veneer and eclectic architectural detailing are successfully blended with Tudor Revival-style elements."

According to Ila, it has been visited by about 250 tourists during a 1988 Christmas home tour, sponsored by the Walker County Historical

The Willhoite House, now owned by Louis and Ila Gaines, is "the most outstanding masonry, revival-styled dwelling in Huntsville," according to a historical survey.
Richard Nira/The Huntsville Item

The Willhoite House's living room features an original rock fireplace the Willhoite family built with rocks picked up on vacations; antique furniture which once belonged to the home's previous owner also adorns the living room.
Richard Nira/The Huntsville Item

WILLHOITE
Continued from Page 1A

told in the "Historic Resources Survey," goes like this: In 1938, O.A. and Edith Willhoite saw a rock house in Austin. They liked it so much that they decided to obtain the plans and build an almost exact replica in Huntsville under the direction of Willhoite's brother, Paul Willhoite.

The story ends happily when the Willhoites moved to Austin in 1945 only to purchase and live in the original rock house. Since then, the Willhoite House changed hands until it wound up under the ownership of Mrs. L.A. Northington. Ila explained that she and Lewis purchased the house in 1970 from Northington's heir, Alma Rankins, after Northington's death.

Ila enjoys telling the story of how Lewis fell in love with the house. Lewis' father was a carpenter, but he also worked at Texaco's Fuller Earth Plant in Riverside, where Willhoite was the general manager. When Lewis was 13, he and his father came to the house to paint the trim.

"He thought this was the most wonderful, most beautiful house he could ever own," Ila said, "so it was sort of a nostalgic trip when we bought it."

The Willhoites had the house constructed of rock imported from west Texas. This rock, which is pieced together like an intricate puzzle, includes fossilized rock and petrified wood for variety. Architectural features built into the house include window ledges made of large pieces of petrified wood, rock window boxes and a brick front doorway and chimney.

The house features interesting shapes as well. For instance, it has very steep, slightly curved A-frame roofs, arched doors, windows and garage doors, and an arched breezeway.

Ila noted that there was no wood used in the construction of the house — something that posed great difficulties when the Gaineses began renovations,

Although the style was popular in special for its local location and place- Ball, the namesake of Tomball, he

especially when installing modern necessities like central air conditioning and TV and phone cables. She still laughs about the number of bits which were burned up in trying to drill through the thick walls.

Upon entering the home, one notices the off-white wall paneling. Ila explained that this was the original pressed fiberboard which was used for heavy insulation. This paneling still remains in the living room, dining room, music room, staircase and halls, as does all the original woodwork.

Particularly interesting in the living room is the original rock fire place. Ila said this was made of items the Willhoite family picked up on vacations, such as petrified wood, fossilized rocks, granite, fool's gold, an arrowhead and an Apache tear.

The living room, which is bedecked in green and burgundy trim, also features antique furniture which once belonged to Northington. Ila explained that she decorated the house in an eclectic style, mingling the modern luxuries with dark wood antiques, Victorian floral prints, and off-white French provincial pieces throughout.

"We wanted the house to be warm and just say 'welcome' when you came in," she said. "That's the mood we tried to create with our decorating."

The downstairs also features a TV room (once the music room), a dining room, a lavender floral bedroom, and a small pink floral bathroom. Ila pointed out with some irritation her only disappointment with the house — the small bathrooms which were common in 1934. She said renovating them was a nightmare because they contained huge bathtubs which were embedded in thick tile flooring and too large to fit through the door.

The Gaineses totally remodeled the kitchen. Today it is decorated in a country style with solid oak floors. It also contains an oak rocking chair which came with the house. The chair is held together by pegs; it was hand-hewn and hand-carved by

prison craftsmen, Ila said.

In 1976, the Gaineses built a sun room onto the back of the house.

"It took a long time to find someone who was even willing to attempt to build a room on," Ila explained. "Everyone said it can't be done."

Again, the rock walls posed problems, as the contractors feared the difficulties of attaching onto rock, but eventually the family got its sun room, which utilizes the outside rock wall of the house as one of the interior walls of the room. This addition also required moving the patio which, like other walkways around the house, is made out of the rocks imported from west Texas in 1934.

Ila said they tried to make the sun room, which is the family's favorite room in the house, match the rest of the house as much as possible. They even went so far as to have jalousie windows specially built for the sun room to match the original windows, she said. These consist of several small panes of glass set in metal.

Once the tourist has climbed the original wooden staircase to the second-floor landing, Ila's nostalgia corner appears. Sitting on an antique marble-top washing stand are old pictures of family members, as well as personal items which belonged to her parents and date back to the World War I era, she said.

The Gaines' master bedroom, which is decorated in yellow and blue florals, also contains antique pictures handed down by Ila's mother. The room features spacious walk-in closets, all lined with the original cedar.

The upstairs also contains another small bathroom, a bedroom and a sitting room which holds all of the family's souvenirs from vacations.

"It's been a really neat house to live in," Gaines said. However, she still remembers the difficulties involved in remodeling this labor of love and added a word of advice: "You have to have a love for old homes. You have to have some imagination and a lot of hard work to restore one."

A 1999 newspaper article in the *The Huntsville Item* described the home.

The Willhoite home with a mantle of snow in this family photo

Family photos and clippings courtesy of the Willhoites and *The Huntsville Item*

232 • Stone-Tree Houses of Texas

OLD TIME TEXAS CHRISTMAS CELEBRATION
HUNTSVILLE, TEXAS

2nd ANNUAL CHRISTMAS HOME TOUR
SATURDAY, DECEMBER 3, 1988
11:00 a.m. – 5:00 p.m.

GUIDE TO A FESTIVE WEEK OF EVENTS
THURSDAY, DECEMBER 1st
through
THURSDAY, DECEMBER 8th

A flyer for the 1988 'Old Time Texas Christmas Celebration' describes the Willhoite House, one of the houses featured in Huntsville's annual Christmas Home Tour.

The Willhoite home appeared again in The Huntsville Item in 2004.

"A GOLDEN CHRISTMAS"
HOME OF MR. AND MRS. LEWIS H. GAINES
1300 AVENUE P

This two story rock house was originally built by O.A. Willhoite and his wife, Edith. Paul Willhoite brother of O.A. was the contractor.

In a letter received from Julie Oliphint Willhoite she relates the following: "O.A. and his wife had seen a rock house in Austin which they liked at 1416 Newfield Lane. They secured the plans, made some changes, and built the rock house in Huntsville. Plans for the house were completed on June 3, 1938 and the building permit was issued on June 30, 1938. The house was completed sometime in October of the same year. The rocks used in the house were selected from somewhere in West Texas. O.A. and his family moved from Huntsville to Austin in 1945 and purchased the house they had copied on Newfield Lane."

The house has had several owners and was purchased from Alma Rankin, the heir of Mrs. L.A. Northington by Lewis and Ila Gaines in 1970.

Some few changes have been made with the addition of a sun room and renovation of the interior. Lewis and Ila have chosen to decorate the house with memorabilia that is meaningful to them. They have combined some antiques that belonged to their families with an accumulation of treasures gathered from their travels to create a nostalgic atmosphere.

This Christmas they have chosen the Golden Christmas theme in celebration of the fiftieth year of the building of the house.

Their towering Christmas tree is decorated with handmade items created by their daughter, Carolyn and their daughter-in-law, Mary. The gold and white theme has been carried out throughout the house and also in the outdoor decorations.

The guest apartment that is connected to the house will also be open for viewing.

Willhoite-Gaines House

8 THE HUNTSVILLE ITEM — **HISTORIC HOMES** — **SUNDAY, JANUARY 25, 2004**

Hidden behind the oldest and largest magnolia trees in town is the Willhoite House, a two-story rock house with Tudor Revival stylistic features owned by Lewis and Ila Gaines, which sits on an acre of land where 13th Street dead-ends into Avenue P.

The house was built in 1938 and is still going strong after nearly 70 years. A few upgrades here and there have kept the house in good condition. The latest addition was roof on the back patio.

"We've done nothing to the integrity of the house over the years," Gaines said. The style is still the same."

The Willhoite House was featured in the City of Huntsville-commissioned "Historic Resources Survey of Huntsville, Texas" by Hardy-Heck-Moore and Dan Utley. The house was referred to as "certainly the most outstanding masonry, revival-styled dwelling in Huntsville."

In 1938, O.A. and Edith Willhoite saw a rock house in Austin they liked and to obtained the plans. The almost exact replica was built here under the direction of Willhoite's brother, Paul Willhoite.

The Willhoite House changed hands until it wound up under the ownership of Mrs. L.A. Northington. The Gaines family purchased the house in 1970 from Northington's heir, Alma Rankins, after Northington's death.

The Willhoites constructed the home of rock imported from West Texas in 1934, which is pieced together like an intricate puzzle. Fossilized rock and petrified wood were included for variety. Architectural features built into the house include window ledges made of large pieces of petrified wood, rock window boxes and a brick front doorway and chimney.

The house has steep, slightly curved A-frame roofs, arched doors, windows and garage doors and an arched breezeway.

No wood was used in the construction of the house — something that posed great difficulties when the Gaines family began renovations, especially when installing modern necessities like central air conditioning and TV and phone cables.

The off-white wall paneling, the original pressed fiberboard used for heavy insulation, remains in some areas, as does all the original woodwork.

Particularly interesting in the living room is the original rock fire place made of items the Willhoite family picked up on vacations, such as petrified wood, fossilized rocks, granite, fool's gold, an arrowhead and an Apache tear.

The downstairs also features a TV room (once the music room), a dining room, a bedroom and a smaller bathroom. Gaines pointed out with some irritation her only disappointment with the house — the small bathrooms which were common in 1934. She said renovating them was a nightmare because they contained huge bathtubs which were embedded in thick tile flooring and too large to fit through the door.

The Gaines family totally remodeled the kitchen. Today, it is decorated in a country style with solid oak floors.

In 1976, the Gaines family built a sun room onto the back of the house, which utilizes the outside rock wall of the house as one of the interior walls of the room.

This addition also required moving the patio which, like other walkways around the house, is made out of imported rocks.

Gaines said they tried to make the sun room, which is the family's favorite room in the house, match the rest of the house as much as possible. Jalousie windows specially built for the sun room to match the original windows were created.

The original wooden staircase leads to the second-floor landing. The upstairs includes The Gaines' master bedroom, another small bathroom, a bedroom and a sitting room.

Members of the Willhoite family enjoy the home and grounds in these family photos

Southeastern Region 233

Southern Region

(CONTINUED FROM PG. 165)

About the Geology

In addition to the above towns, also located within the Yegua are (from north to south) Crockett, Madisonville, Bryan/College Station, and Giddings (Barnes, 1992), and each of these towns are known hotspots for fossil wood collecting, with large logs in yards and flower beds as well as in hobbyists' collections.

The Yegua Formation was deposited during a thermal maximum, which means that absolute temperatures were higher than they had been since the Mesozoic Age (Graham, 1999). It was drier than during Wilcox Group times, so the species assemblage consisted of a drier-tropical mix of angiosperms (hardwoods) and gymnosperms (softwoods). The variety of species represented is substantial, indicating an extremely diverse forest existed at that time.

In the upper Eocene (~41-38 m.y.) there are a number of thin formations that are all lumped into the Jackson Group (Whitsett, Manning, Wellborn, and Cadell Formations). Of these the first two are terrigenous and are wood producers. Another fluvial formation (the Oligocene Catahoula Formation, ~33-17 m.y.) lies above the upper Eocene Jackson Group and is a known producer of very silicified and opalized wood. All of these formations are known to collectors but generally are not thick enough to be used for building materials. The only houses located on this group of formations are in Sommerville.

The Miocene Fleming Formation (~17-5 m.y.) and the Pliocene Willis Formation (~2 m.y.) are both known to locally produce wood, sometimes abundantly. The houses in Huntsville, Brenham, and Columbus are built on these formations, however it is very possible that wood was transported from the more prolific Eocene to use as building material.

East Texas has an abundance of fossil wood in the basal portion of the Fleming Formation. The house in Jasper was built using this material, as well as a number of walls, flower beds, etc., in this area. Several houses in adjacent portions of Louisiana have been built with the same type of material.

Petrified wood from the Catahoula Formation, Oligocene Age, around Sam Rayburn Reservoir north of Jasper, is known for its great abundance of silicified wood. The silica and mineral impurities (for color) come from volcanic ash originating from west Texas during that time.

Palm is common in the Catahoula, but it gets picked up as soon as

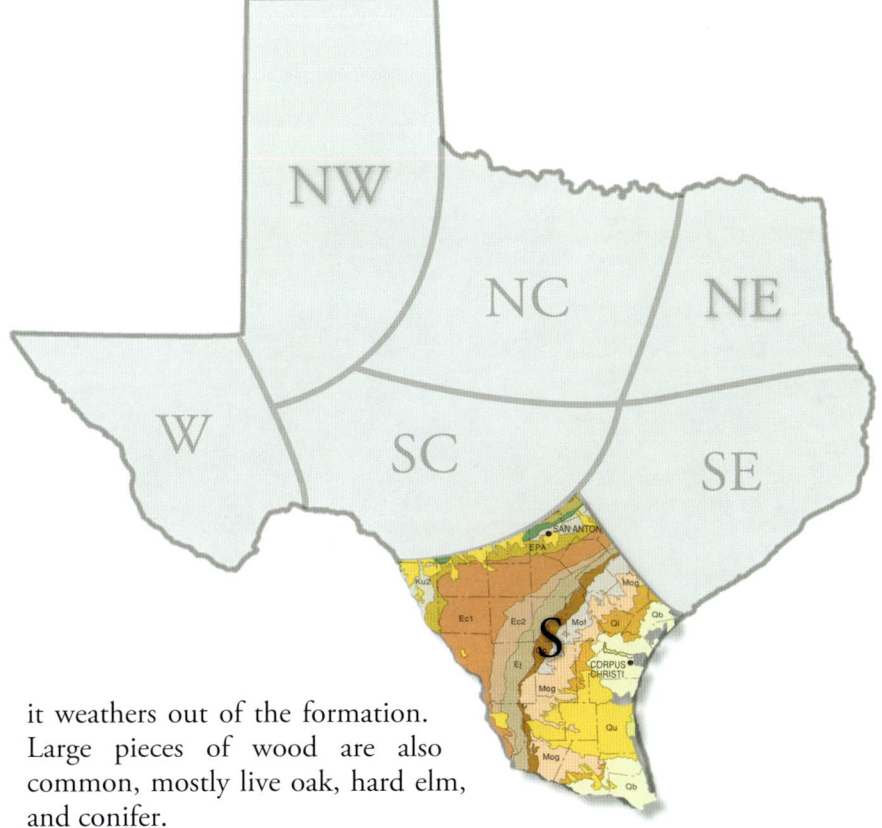

it weathers out of the formation. Large pieces of wood are also common, mostly live oak, hard elm, and conifer.

The reason fossil wood is prevalent in the Miocene in this area is because the primary depocenter, or loci where large rivers transport sediment from the Rocky Mountains, shifted over geologic time from the central Texas coast to east Texas and then into Louisiana, eventually shifting eastward to the current Mississippi River floodplain (Galloway, et al, 2000).

During the Miocene, the depocenter was in western Louisiana, spilling over into east Texas. With this large influx of sediment came the same kinds of depositional environments that existed during the Eocene in Texas when bountiful amounts of wood were buried and fossilized.

Finally, several petrified wood houses are located in coastal portions of central Texas (Houston, Brookshire, and Garwood).

All of these houses were built with transported material from inland locations, likely from nearby Miocene or Eocene formations.

— *Scott Singleton*

San Antonio: Nowotny House

The Nowotny House nestles amongst live oaks atop a hill in San Antonio (Bexar County). The house grew out of a rock collection started by Monroe Nowotny in the early 1930s. Mrs. Nowotny says they collected rocks for years, moving them five times before using them in the construction of their house.

The home's veneer combines different types of stone from all over the world, including fossils and petrified wood, many contributed by friends and family.

A metal arch listing the names of family members — Monroe, Evelyn, Texas, Ben and Dale — spanned the original stone and fossil wood entry to the Nowotny House; it was demolished when the road was widened.

HOME OF THE WEEK

Here's a House That Rocks Built

By CYNTHIA VOLLMER

An interesting hobby became a haven for the family of Mr. and Mrs. Monroe Nowotny. Their home at 8823 Kenney Road is built of unusual rocks from around the globe.

Mr. Nowotny says it all started with a small rock collection that just grew and grew and grew. The rocks represent every state and about 20 countries. In the walls of this home are fossils, petrified wood, rock from Gibralter — even a piece of rock from the Great Wall of China.

The rocks in this house are so varied that over the years groups of geology students from St. Mary's University have visited the Nowotny home on field trips.

Built on eight-and-one half acres, this home reflects the varied interests of each person in the Nowotny family. Mr. and Mrs. Nowotny and their children, Texas, Ben and Dale, gathered around a table and each told the architect what they wanted in the home. Texas and Ben are now married and have homes of their own, but often bring their families by the house for visits.

Half-And-Half

At first Mrs. Nowotny wasn't sure she would like a home built of so many different kinds of stone. So they built the bottom half of the house first. After seeing how it would look, they completed the rest of the building.

Although rocks of many shades make up this beautiful home, it has a very definite rose hue, and Mrs. Nowotny has used shades of rose and pink to decorate the entrance, the living room and dining room.

In the living room a contemporary divided sofa of turquoise and white brocade compliments the dusty pink drapes and carpet. A louvered wall creates the effect of a separate room for the dining area and at the same time gives the feeling of continuity.

Focal Point

The living room opens into the den, the focal point of the Nowotny home. Dominating this room is the magnificent rock fireplace, which contains uncut semi-precious stones, such as garnets and amethyst. The fireplace also contains a walrus tusk, rare petrified palm wood, leaf fossils, bayrite, gold ore, rose quartz and a large sea fossil dug up in Nowotny's lawn.

Redwood paneling sets the western theme of the room and a wagon wheel fixture lights the redwood ceiling beams. A contemporary couch and chair are combined with an original Frederick horn chair made in the 1880's and a round table set with polished stones.

To the left of the den is a bar area which opens into the kitchen. Aqua tile and beach wood cabinets make the compact modern kitchen a

San Antonio EXPRESS/NEWS — Sunday, July 26, 1964

The Nowotnys on the front terrace of their spacious home. The house's picture windows look over a valley toward city skyline.

The *San Antonio Express-News* featured articles on the Nowotny House several times over the years.

Family photos and clippings courtesy of the Nowotnys and the *San Antonio Express-News*

Rockhound's Dream House

By JUNE KILSTOFTE

ALL SORTS of people like to collect rocks, possibly because they're such easy things to latch on to. You just go walking, stub your toe, and there you are.

The one drawback to the hobby is that rocks are not the easiest thing in the world to display. Sooner or later you run out of cabinets, and the first thing you know, you've got a rock pile in the backyard.

Monroe Nowotny solved the problem neatly. He built himself a house — a spacious home high on a hill that is truly a rockhound's dream house.

For in the walls are dozens of types of rock — sandstone, calcite, quartz, gypsum, fluorspar, feldspar, hematite, petrified woods. There are the desert roses which so resemble their namesakes, and fossilized leaves and fish and crustaceans.

The rocks come from all over the world. There's one from each of the 48 states — some of them from such places as Grand Coulee Dam, Death Valley, Pikes Peak, Mount Rushmore — and some from foreign countries. There's a rock from the Rock of Gibralter, one from the Sphinx, another from the Morro Castle in Cuba. Mount Suribachi yielded one specimen, Paricutin Volcano, the Carthage ruins, the House of Parliament, others.

The whole thing started back about 1935, when Nowotny first started collecting rocks. He traveled a lot, and everywhere he went, he picked up, bought, or traded rocks.

He remembers his first trip to Arkansas, back in 1938. "They've got so many kinds of rock up there," he says, "I almost went crazy. We had a stationwagon, and before we knew it, there was no room for our luggage. It ended up with us having to ship some of the rocks back to Texas."

Along with collecting himself, Nowotny soon found his friends were collecting for him. "Send me a rock," he asked, when he heard his friends were taking a trip. All of them obliged.

One G.I. who was heading for Puerto Rico was more than obliging. Most people sent back a small rock; the G.I. sent off a boulder, collect. The express charges were $12.

Some of the nicest specimens in the house, Nowotny says, were collected by a government trapper over a two year period. He stashed away the rocks in arroyos and canyons, finally asked Nowotny to come pick up the rocks. They covered a wide area, came back with a trailer-full.

Nowotny's first idea, as the rockpile began growing, was to build a museum alongside a business he had. The war interfered. Then the business was sold. So the Nowotnys decided they would build a house with their rock. They began their project last May, finished the house in November.

Their seven-room home, of modern design, is perched on a hill on Kenney Road at Ridge Road. In the distance is the San Antonio skyline.

Every inch of wall outside is actually an exhibit piece. And Nowotny can tell you what every piece is, and, in most cases, where it came from.

There was little difficulty in building this very different rock house, he says. The rocks were sorted out before building, and varieties that would look good side by side where chosen. Both Mr. and Mrs. Nowotny, who like her husband is a rockhound, lent a hand with the placing of some of the rocks.

Some of the choicer items were saved for the fireplace in the den. Among other things, there is gold and silver ore, turquoise, a chunk from the white cliffs of Dover.

The outside barbecue pit is of rock, too. Prize item there is a dinosaur track, picked up in Arizona.

And Nowotny still has rock left over. It's going to go into a friendship wall across the front of his place.

"You bet I'm going to keep on collecting," he says firmly. "That's going to be a long wall."

The large fossil fish points to the doorbell.

"Got petrified ram's horn," someone claimed. It was a crustacean.

S. A. 'Rockhounds' Build Own Unique House

By MARJORIE CLAPP

What do you do with a pile of rocks?

Build a house, of course.

At least, that's what the Monroe Nowotnys did with tons stacked in their back yard.

And thanks to such unique taste, their rambling hilltop home is perhaps the most unusual house in San Antonio.

For in the walls are dozens of types of rock—sandstone, calcite, quartz, gypsum, feldspar, hematite and 40 tons of petrified woods—from all over the world.

OPALS FROM MEXICO

There are desert roses which so resemble their namesakes, and fossilized leaves and fish and crustaceans. Wedged between the rocks of an inside fireplace are opals from Australia and Mexico, deep-red garnet, some 50 truckloads were hauled to the hilltop spot from a site on Broadway.

Built four years ago, the house has specimens in it from each of the 48 states and 16 foreign countries. Later, 600 feet of rock fencing were added.

Some of the rocks are rare. For example, in the fence are rocks from War Correspondent Ernie Pyle's grave, the birthplace of General MacArthur and Hiroshima, where the first atom bomb was dropped.

Those and other foreign rocks from such places as the Great Wall of China, the Pyramids, Morro Castle in Cuba, Mount Suribachi and the White Cliffs of Dover are gifts from Nowotny friends.

NATIVE SAMPLES

But the couple gathered the native samples.

Some dinosaur tracks at the back of the house were chiseled out of an Arizona rockbed in rocks are two large sections of crystalized calcite from the only deposit known in Texas.

According to Nowotny, the substance is used for optical lenses, and sells for about $25 a pound. His rocks total about 100 pounds.

ROUND PATIO TABLE

But more prized is a simple slab of limestone adorned with a painting of a cowboy by Ad Toepperwein, world-famous rifle and pistol shot.

Latest addition to the household is a round den or patio table of polished stone from four foreign countries and four states.

That used up a good part of the remaining collection. But the couple has trips for years to come planned.

And what'll they do with rocks now?

It's simple, says Nowotny:

"We'll build another fence."

Evelyn Nowotny relaxes in the living room

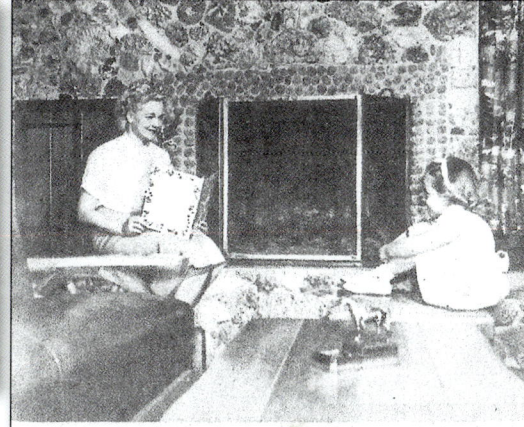

Before the fireplace in the den, Mrs. Nowotny reads a story to daughter Dale. Edging the fireplace are rows of "desert roses."

"ROCKHOUND" MONROE NOWOTNY SHOWS OFF HIS UNIQUE FIREPLACE
House is built of rocks from 48 states and 16 foreign countries.

Another *San Antonio Express-News* article described Mr. Nowotny's dream house.

Southern Region 239

Monroe Nowotny and his son, Monroe, Jr., get ready for big barbecue.

The chimney, covered with exotic rocks sent to the Nowotnys from every state and 20 countries, faces the back yard. The dinosaur footprint (below) was excavated by the Nowotnys during a trip to Arizona.

240 • *Stone-Tree Houses of Texas*

Several examples of stonework from the Nowotny House

Southern Region 241

Seguin: Pape House

A bungalow-style guest cottage is the smallest of the three original structures.

Three structures are original to the Pape property – two homes and a three-car garage with an apartment above – all built in the late 1930s on two large lots in Seguin (Guadalupe County). Each features highly detailed stone and fossil wood exteriors and decorative ironwork.

They belonged to Walter Pape, a parts manager of Lovett Motors in Seguin who also worked for the fire department from 1946 to 1951. He was a cousin to the Hornungs in Lexington (pg. 178). His wife Leonie (McGee) taught piano and played the organ.

The three-car garage has an apartment above and was built first.

Walter Pape, Seguin Fire Chief

Black and white image courtesy of the Seguin Heritage Museum

Southern Region 243

The two-story Pape main house shows the only stone tree house found which has more petrified wood applied to the back than to the front.

The garage apartment on the Pape property

Side elevation of the main building

Spanish-style roof tiles form an unusual decorative gable vent.

The two-story Spanish/Mediterranean-styled house faces the street. It is one of the three separate structures original to the property.

The guest house is the smallest and newest building on the property, built after 2000.

Spanish-style tiles cap the colorful entryway of the larger two story residence

Adams Gardens Entry Gates

Adams Gardens was an early master-planned community begun in 1931 in Cameron County and promoted by developer Charles Ladd. Originally intended to accommodate hundreds of homes, the development stalled due to a downturn in the economy and only 18 homes were ever built on the site. The finished houses were built entirely out of concrete and were topped with tile roofs; although the homes themselves were not stone-tree houses, a few did feature petrified wood fireplaces.

Additionally the developers built four large stone and fossil wood entrance gates along U.S. Route 83 and several ornamental posts columns still remain scattered throughout the subdivision. Carved sandstone figures of people and animals decorate the elaborate columns interspersed with colorful stones and large pieces of fossil wood.

Developer Charles Ladd offered something for everyone with his pitches for Adams Gardens; the developer tempted potential owners to make their home 'in a land of orange blossoms, palms and poinsettias' and boasts of Adams Gardens' location 'In the Valley of Golden Grapefruit.' Options for the prospective buyer ran the gamut from 'little cottages and bungalows' to Spanish-style 'pretentious mansions.'

Costume details are expressed in petrified wood and carved stone set into the end of the curved entry wall.

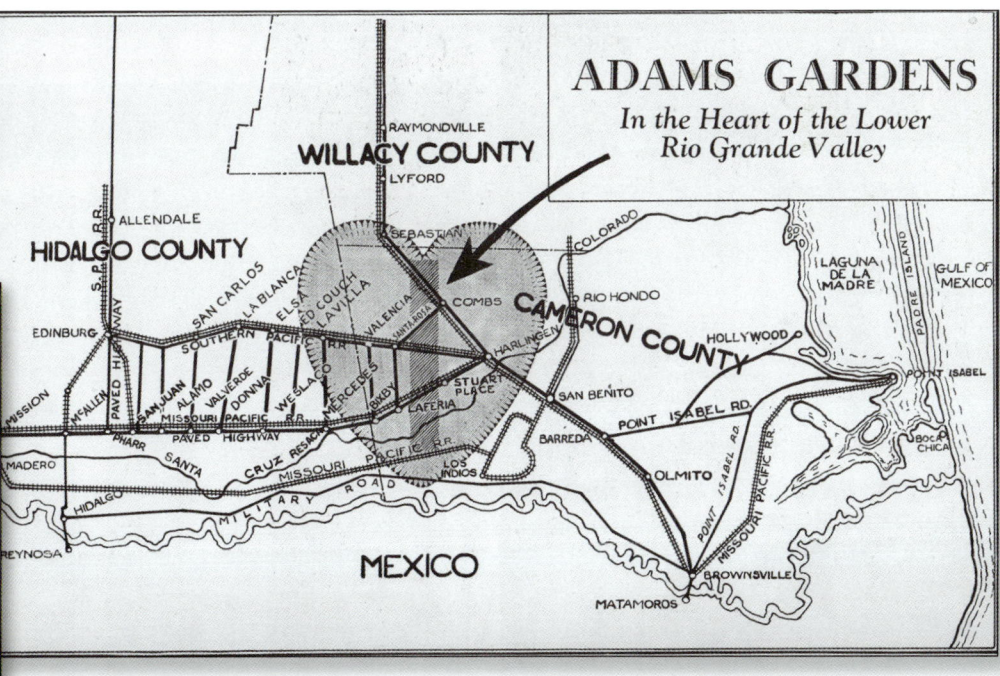

1930s-era promotional materials for Adams Gardens described the new development and provided a map of the location in the 'Heart of the Lower Rio Grande Valley.'

Southern Region 247

Elaborate fossil wood and stone columns and gateways are scattered throughout the planned development with many featuring faces of people and animals carved in a rustic style from solid stone. At least two are dated 1931.

248 • *Stone-Tree Houses of Texas*

GENERAL TOPICS

PETRIFIED FOREST.

In the vicinity of Roma in Starr County, there is an interesting deposit of gigantic petrified oyster shells and petrified trees. The oyster shells are in mounds, proving that this section was at one time under the sea. Some of the petrified shells are well preserved and are over eighteen inches in diameter.

The petrified trees are really only stumps and parts of the trees. There are no complete tree trunks, although the roots and branches of the trees are clearly defined in the parts which remain. They are not of the present local woods, mesquite or ebony, but of some far larger varieties of wood. Some of the stumps indicate that the trees were more than four feet in diameter. The color and grain of the wood suggest several different varieties of trees. Some years ago a petrified pecan nut one-inch long and a half-inch in diameter was found among the petrified tree deposits. As the pecan is a semi-tropical nut its appearance with the petrified trees suggest that these also were semi-tropical. Although it is entirely possible that the remains of these petrified trees came from an existing forest on the banks of the Rio Grande, it is more probable that they were brought down stream after the great glacial slide and deposited in the back waters of a great inland lake or bay extending up into Starr County from the Gulf of Mexico. The evidence of the oyster shells close to where the petrified wood is found indicates that the water covering that section was salt or sea water.

The age of the petrified deposits has been variously estimated by scientists who have examined these formations. Some say that they are over forty million years old, but on this matter we have no authentic information and do not care to hazard a guess. Nor would it be possible to offer proof regarding the varieties of woods found in the petrified forest. One stump of a fair sized tree has the outward appearance of bamboo. It has been asserted that there are some bamboo woods among those found in this ancient deposit. But as already stated, we do not have authentic information and do not make claims for the suggestions noted here.

An excerpt from the 1931 book, *The Lower Rio Grande Valley of Texas and Its Builders* compiled by Mrs. James Watson of Mission, describes a large deposit of fossil wood in the Rio Grande Valley near Roma, considered to be the source of the fossil wood used in Adams Gardens as well as in the Cummings' house at Donna (pg. 250).

DONNA: THE CUMMINGS HOUSE

The tinted, panoramic images of the Cummings House are dated 1930 and were found rolled in a tube in the attic by a former owner.

> There is a picturesque and very substantial house belonging to Mr. and Mrs. R. Cummings on the old Pomeroy Place, about one mile east of Donna, Texas, which is built of petrified trees taken from the petrified forest near Roma. Some of the pieces of petrified tree trunks weigh between four and five hundred pounds. The cement in which they are set had to be supported with field stones and allowed to harden several hours to form a foundation for these heavy pieces of petrified wood.
>
> When the house was first planned the intention was to use petrified wood on the corners only. But the effect produced by this beautiful formation was so entirely satisfactory that it was decided to build the walls of the house from petrified wood. It was a big undertaking, requiring hauling for more than five months and employing five trucks to bring the pieces used in the building. The utmost care was used in setting the petrified wood so that the grain would show to advantage. The pieces were left in their original condition and they produce an effect altogether pleasing and unique.
>
> The interior of the house carries out the scheme of the builder. The ceilings have heavy hand-hewn rafters of natural wood. The floors are finished in wide planking of highly polished natural wood finish. The hardware is of hand-hammered brass, as are the lighting fixtures. The curtain rods are of hand-worked spear heads. There is an interior pool, made entirely of selected pieces of petrified wood, the water playing in various colors from an unusual indirect lighting arrangement.
>
> This house reflects the fine spirit of hospitality and home-like atmosphere with which one is so happily impressed when a guest within its doors.

Laborers in the lower Rio Grande Valley prepare a building site using a mule team and a grading device known as a 'fresno.'

These two excerpts from the 1931 book *The Lower Rio Grande Valley of Texas and Its Builders* compiled by Mrs. James Watson of Mission, offers theories about the origins of the petrified forest near Roma. The article then describes in detail the construction of the Cummings' house, built with fossil wood from the deposit.

The tinted photos are courtesy of Dorothea Nell Nollkamper and her son Wade; Additional archival material courtesy of George Gause, University of Texas Pan America Library, Edinburg

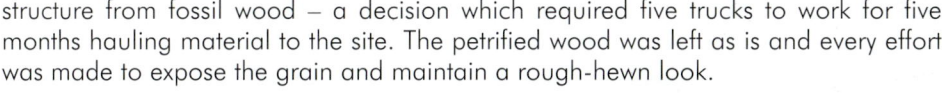

According to Mrs. Watson's book, the builders of the Cummings House originally intended to use petrified wood from the Roma 'petrified forest' only to accent the corners of the structure but so liked the effect that they decided to build the entire structure from fossil wood – a decision which required five trucks to work for five months hauling material to the site. The petrified wood was left as is and every effort was made to expose the grain and maintain a rough-hewn look.

In addition to an actual fireplace (left), what appears to be a second fireplace and hearth (at right) in fact encloses an indoor waterfall in the Cummings House. Mrs. Watson wrote of the home: 'There is an interior pool, made entirely of selected pieces of petrified wood, the water playing in various colors from an indirect lighting arrangement.'

A singular tile appears amidst a field of red tile in the foyer floor. Other details include the old house number found in a cement window sill.

One of the hand-colored photographs shows a reflecting pool surrounded by lilies.

Another 1930 panoramic image of the house and gardens of Mr. and Mrs. R.E. Cummings shows a more complete view of the original landscaping and grounds, which then included orchards, a colonnaded arbor, rock columns, planters, benches and cobblestone curbs lining a circular entry drive.

Appendix A

Petrified Wood Colors and Petrification

Red and Pink colors are produced by the presence of hematite, a form of oxidized iron - Fe_2O_3. The intensity of the color depends on the quantity of hematite present in the petrified wood.
Process: Iron dissolves in ground water when no oxygen is present. The ground water becomes re-oxygenated as it moves though the tree trunks causing oxygen to bond with the iron. The iron then precipitates to produce a solid form of iron called hematite. This hematite is incorporated into the log's cell walls. The same process occurs when iron stains porcelain sinks. The soluble iron in ground water becomes oxidized into a solid form when it comes in contact with air, causing a reddish stain.
Yellow, Brown and Orange colors are produced by the presence of goethite – $HFeO_2$ and Fe_2O_3. Goethite is a hydrated iron oxide that is derived by weathering from iron bearing minerals. It crystallizes into tablets, scales, needles, radial and concentric aggregates.
Green-colored petrified wood is produced by pure reduced iron that is a magnetic, malleable mineral. The chemical composition is Fe. Referred to as native iron, it is quite rare in terrestrial rocks but common in meteorites. Native iron combines with chlorophyll to give tree leaves and plants their green colors but rarely attaches to wood cells.
White is produced by pure silica – SiO_2. Since silicon, Si, and oxygen, O, are the two most abundant elements in the earth's crust. Silica group minerals are common worldwide. Free silica, SiO_2, referred to scientifically as silicon dioxide, occurs most commonly as quartz. Quartz is the principal element of glass. In many respects quartz is the most interesting of all minerals. It has a larger number of distinct varieties with wider differences than any other mineral.

Petrified wood, also referred to as silicified wood, is a common illustration of a quartz pseudomorph – wood is slowly replaced, cell by cell, by silica, until not a trace of the original material remains.
Process: The structural arrangement of silicon and oxygen creates an open bonding structure that permits other ions such as various forms of iron to occupy interstitial positions in the molecule and bond to it, thus producing variations in color.
Black – Organic carbon or pyrite - FeS_2 (iron sulfide), the most abundant and widespread sulfide mineral, produces black. Because it was mistaken for gold it is often called "fool's gold." Pyrite, translated freely, means "fire mineral," a reference to the sparks given off when struck.
Process: The wood was affected as hydrogen sulfide from decaying organic matter interacted with iron forming pyrite.
Purple and Blue are produced by manganese dioxide – MnO_2. This is a secondary material formed when water leaches manganese from igneous rock and re-deposits it as a concentration of manganese dioxide. As a result, it occurs more often as coatings on other minerals than as large crystals. Manganese is very important in the manufacture of steel.
Tan indicates silica dioxide is the predominate replacement mineral. This color is most often seen in permineralized wood. In permineralization, the wood's cell structure is better preserved, giving it the appearance of real wood. It should be noted that not all petrified wood in the park is permineralized. Permineralization also transpires when wood is preserved with calcite rather than silica. No calcified wood occurs in the park.
How the very fine detail of the cell structure is preserved is not well understood. It would appear that less than cell-sized gradients in acidity created very small reprecipitation gradients, replacing the wood on almost an atom by atom basis.

This colorful petrified wood log is from the Canadian River area of the Texas Panhandle. The fossil wood from this area is valued for its bright colors.

Appendix B

Site Status and Preservation Prospects

Amarillo
McCollum House: Well-built, owner-occupied and located in established historic neighborhood. The present condition is good, future outlook also good.
Heath House: Well-built property in historic university neighborhood, present condition good, prospects for preservation good.

Alanreed
Bruce Nursery: Private residence, no longer operating as a business. The beautiful setting and rural area combined with sound original construction make continued preservation likely.

Canyon
Buffalo Courts: Historic recognition by state historic commission, WTA&M University and present occupant, University Alumni Association, gives the Buffalo Court the best possible outlook for short and long term preservation.

Matador
Bob's Cook Shack: Although vacant and boarded up after owner Bob Robertson's death in 1947, recent recognition by Texas Historical Commission, efforts by local residents and solid construction make long term preservation promising. Still owned by Robertson family.

Abernathy
Shadden: Working farm and house still owned and occupied by family. Sandy Caprock soil has created some cracks in mortar due to settling, but short term prospects are good, long term hopeful but unknown.
Anderson: On main street and farm-to-market road intersection, owner-occupied and in excellent condition, long term prospects are good.

Anton
Brazil house: Located on working farm and recently reconditioned by present owners prospects for short and long term preservation are good.

Idalou
Knoles: Recognized as endangered when located, house has since been demolished.

Lubbock
Fisher/Huffstedler: Well-built and well-maintained in a nice neighborhood of similar vintage, short and long term prospects for preservation very good.
Brunson: Owner occupied, originally constructed on dirt road outside town, now an urban farm-to-market surrounded by newer housing development, prospects very good.

Acuff
Moore: A part of the Moore's family farm headquarters area but unoccupied for some years, well-built, farm still operated by the family so preservation prospects are hopeful but uncertain.

Rotan
Vittitow: Owner-occupied, good condition and not threatened by development; safe for the foreseeable future.

Snyder
King: New owner-occupants have reconditioned to very comfortable and tasteful modern living condition, preservation prospects are very good.

Alpine
Walker: Owner-occupied in university area and not likely to be affected by urban development, this house should remain in its present state of good preservation for a very long time.

Castelon
Dorgan: At the time of acquisition by the National Park system in the 1950s, preservation policies called for "modern" relics of civilization to naturally deteriorate out of existence. A shift in this policy has resulted in the documentation and stabilization of these ruins. The condition of this site is therefore expected to remain the same unless of course there is another change in policy.

Gordon
Ringo: House and ranch still owned and occupied by family, preservation assured for foreseeable future.

Abilene
Shoemaker House: Well maintained and in excellent condition, located in established historic neighborhood making prospects for preservation very good

Glen Rose
Sycamore Grove: The future of this site is much more of a mystery than its past at this point in time, making it impossible to rate the prospects for its preservation. A positive factor is that "it's still there" and appears to be stable for the time being. All other sites in Glen Rose seem to fit into the Petrified City aspect of the civic identity and thanks to the Sommervell County Historical Society, and efforts of concerned citizens, should be safely preserved.

Jacksboro
Nash: House is owner-occupied, well-maintained and well away from the highway, should be safe. Store ruins may be affected by future highway expansion.

Decatur
Texas Tourist Court: Commercially viable as a cafe and office space and far enough off the beaten path to avoid encroachment by commercial development. These factors plus national register status should ensure preservation indefinitely.

Stephenville
Wolfe Nursery: House and nursery demolished for parking lots in the early nineties.
Latham
Owner-occupied in established residential neighborhood not likely to be affected by urban expansion extended preservation likely.

Rising Star
City Hall: Still used as city hall, likely to continue indefinitely.

Dublin
Hudson: Owned and occupied by the family, beautiful setting, set well back from highway, preservation prospects good.
Hughes: Attractive home located on main highway but with adequate set-back to allow for future expansion. Continued preservation likely.

Bronte
Youngblood: Well-maintained and owner occupied. Preservation prospects very good

San Angelo
Jennings: House and commercial property still owned by family, good prospects for preservation.
Young: House remains in the family and continued preservation likely.
Leddy House: House dismantled due to commercial expansion, porch with inlay of boot rebuilt inside Leddy's Bootshop in downtown San Angelo.
Curry House and Curry Wonder Shop: Currently a single family rental property on farm-to-market highway outside of San Angelo does not appear to be in imminent danger of destruction.

Ft. Worth
Williams House: Impeccably maintained, architecturally significant home in an elegant neighborhood, can be expected to remain such for a very long time.
Schnieder/Burger House: House on Burger Lake property and should retain excellent prospects for preservation.
Stevens House: House is now used as a day care center for children and is surrounded by new high end apartment complexes; success as a commercial property should ensure preservation for some time.
Stevens Commercial Building: Recent restoration and its location in historic district should ensure preservation indefinitely.

Colleyville
Black House: Located near the center of now thriving Colleyville. Preservation prospects more uncertain.

Tyler
Smith House: Very attractive house on a "brick street" in the Azelea Historic district, preservation chances very good.

Rusk
Schochler House: Nice house in good neighborhood without commercial development, preservation chances are good.
Austin
Petrified Forest Lodge: Deteriorating condition from deferred maintenance and increasing value as commercial property resulted in its demolition in the 1990s.
Harper
Peril Ranch House: Original ranch has been subdivided among heirs but preservation of house highly likely.
Bandera
Frontier Times Museum: Maintenance declined for building and contents for a period but recent renovations have revived interest and preservation chances are very good.
Lufkin
Read house: Structural problems due to weight of tile roof and commercial development of the surrounding area led to demolition in 1998
Hoyte:
Pressley House: Ownership remains in Pressley family, preservation hopeful.
Lexington
Hornung House: Ranch and house remain in family, preservation hopeful.
Rockdale
Copeland/Fiesler: Striking appearance and superior maintenance to date make preservation chances very high.
Coffield: Now occupied by Rockdale Chamber of Commerce and well maintained; chances for preservation are very high.
Cooks Point
Chaloupka: After numerous renovations this house still stands in the same spot and is likely to remain.
Urbanovsky: Recently renovated and likely to remain for some time.
Drgac: Recent correction of foundation problems should ensure long term preservation.
Brethren Church: Demolished in 1959
Caldwell
Woodson: Striking in appearance, well-located and maintained, preservation appears certain.
Burleson County Fairground Ticket Office: No longer used by county fairgrounds, but likely to be preserved.
Snook
Elsik House: On family farm, the house is likely to be preserved for some time.
Sommerville
Nedbalek House: House now for sale or rent; although future is uncertain, imminent destruction is unlikely.

Brenham
Meyer House: House still owned and occupied by owner, condition of house and nice neighborhood make preservation chances good.
Public cannery: Remains a county property, future use uncertain, but preservation likely.
Columbus
Kerr: Ownership remains with family, well-maintained property will be preserved.
Gonzalez
Halamicek: Current owner has restored and revitalized house and property; preservation chances are very good.
Houston
Helweg: Recent restoration and expansion make preservation likely despite extensive changes to immediate neighborhood.
Brookshire
Longenbaugh/Eve's Garden: Recent refurbishing into a bed and breakfast with a wedding chapel, preservation very likely.
England: Owner-occupied on outskirts of small town preservation seems likely for some time.
Garwood
Zboril: Well maintained and qwner-occupied, located on the edge of small town and continued preservation likely.
Jasper
Munson: Used as offices for accounting firm for several decades, continued preservation very likely.
Huntsville
Willhoite: Beautiful location in older residential area and excellent condition of property make continued preservation of house very likely.
San Antonio
Nowotny: Present owners dedicated to preservation but large lot and urban setting may cast doubt on long term prospects.
Adams Gardens Entry Gates: Located along highway and railroad right-of-way; preservation status and even ownership is unknown.
Donna
Cummings: Condition of property is very good and with restoration efforts ongoing, preservation is very likely.

APPENDIX C

The following is excerpted from Scott Singleton's *Anatomy of Fossil Woods and Paleoclimate in the Texas Gulf Coast Tertiary and Cretaceous: An Ongoing Research Project. Part 2. Methods, Collection and Sampling Procedures* (the study in its entirety is at www.sas.org, *The Citizen Scientist*).

Collection: The process of collecting samples follows one of two well-defined paths (personally collected or donated by a third party). If the samples are personally collected, the locality is either marked with GPS coordinates or on a large-scale (about 1:218,000) county road map. These location points are then transferred to the appropriate 1:250,000 Geological Atlas of Texas sheet for stratigraphic delineation. All locational, stratigraphic, and sample data are recorded on a master Microsoft Excel spreadsheet and subsequently ported to an ArcInfo GIS database for visualization

The second path is when the samples are donated by a third party. In that case stringent requirements are in effect. The owner of the samples must be able to specify an exact or approximately exact location where they were collected, and must be able to verbally assure me that no contamination has taken place between the time they were collected and the time I received them. Even if that information and assurance has been provided, all third party specimens are inspected during evaluation to make sure they appear to be from the same locality and that the specimens match known characteristics of that area or formation. Following this, the specimens are cataloged and recorded as described above.

Specimen Preparation: Following field collection, all specimens are evaluated. The first step is to clean the specimens of all dirt and lichen, by high-pressure wash if necessary. If the specimens have iron or soil staining that can not be easily removed, they are soaked in an oxalic acid bath prior to high pressure wash. Following cleaning, the specimens are checked for fresh cross-sectional exposures. If none exist, one is created with a lapidary saw.

The specimens are then observed under a 6x-31x binocular Wild M7S scope and classified according to macroscopic cellular features. Sometimes this classification is good enough to separate individual genera, but sometimes it is not. This is because separation based on cross-sectional characteristics alone is not always good enough to distinguish genera. For instance, in the specimen pool of this research there are multiple genera, sometimes spread across different families, that have abundant, single-cell-wide, short bands of parenchyma perpendicular to the rays (e.g. tangentially oriented). In these cases, thin section analysis is necessary to separate genera.

The intention of this phase in the evaluation is to separate different classes of samples for further study.

After all samples are classified into groups, they are evaluated again. Poor samples are discarded. The best samples are set aside for thin sectioning. The results are then tabulated to form a temporary diagnosis for the locality.

Thin Sections: Selected specimens have been sent for slide preparation more or less continuously since the inception of this project in 2000. Slides are prepared by professional petrographers with costs covered by myself. (Petrography is the detailed study of rocks via thin section analysis, see http://en.wikipedia.org/wiki/Petrography). In the case of paleobotany, normal mineralogic petrography is melded with the principles of botany to create biological thin sections out of rock material. This entails the creation of standard rock thin sections except the slides are thicker so that the cellular structure can be imaged (I have mine made about 50-70 μ thick), and that three orthogonal sections (transverse, radial, and tangential) need to be made so that all cellular surfaces are imaged. (A good layman's reference on the preparation and use of botanical thin sections can be found in Hoadley, 1990).

To date, about 300 specimens have been thin sectioned. About ¾ of these have all three orthogonal sections, totaling around 700 slides. About 25-100 slides per year are made during the normal course of research activities. I anticipate this rate will be maintained through the life of the project.

Following thin sectioning and documentation in an Excel spreadsheet, all sections are comprehensively photographed to document all relevant cellular features. The usual procedure is to take a series of pictures of each feature, changing the focus point slightly on each picture. Then in photo processing (described below) the non-optimal shots are discarded.

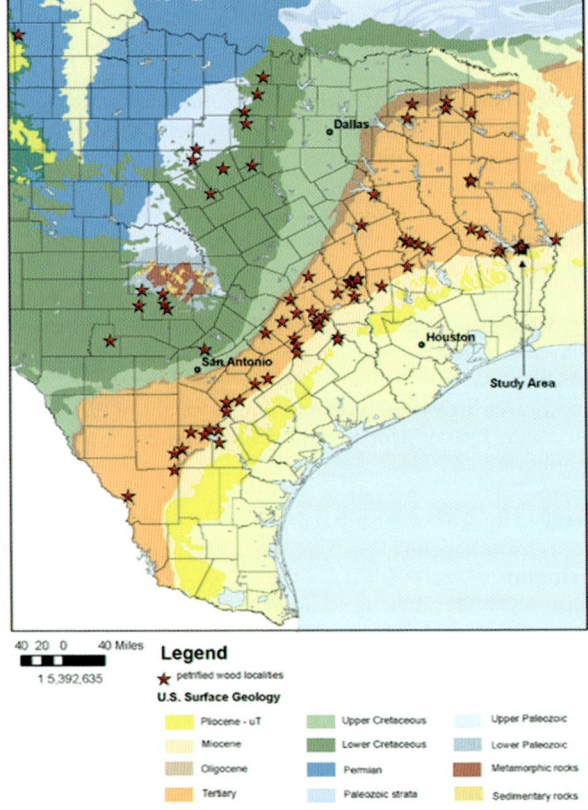

Regional surface geology map showing fossil wood localities the study area in Singleton, 2008. Geologic base map courtesy of the U.S. Geological Survey (see French and Schenk, 2007).

Prior to 2007 the camera system was a Nikon Coolpix 4300 shot through an eyepiece adapter on a Zeiss Photoscope. In 2007 the photo system was revamped. The Zeiss Photoscope was still used, but a phototube was manufactured according to Zeiss standards, above which was placed a Zeiss "C" mount, then a Martin Microscope MM99 adapter, and finally a Canon S5-IS digital camera. Photo magnifications range from 31x to 500x.

Following photography, all pictures are photo processed and cataloged using Adobe Lightroom. This software produces professional-quality photos by managing and editing white balance, saturation, tone, contrast, etc. Lightroom is a companion to Adobe Photoshop but is less expensive and tailored to photographers rather than graphic artists.

Identification of Fossil Woods

The identification of gymnosperm and angiosperm families and genera is primarily done through the use of software for keyed entry followed by pictorial confirmation of possible matches. At the beginning of this study, samples were keyed out using the GUESS program from North Carolina State University (Wheeler, et al, 1986; LaPasha, 1987) which used the OPCN database (Oxford ; Princes Risborough Laboratory, England; Centre Technique Forestier Tropical, France; NC State University).

In the late 1990's, NCSU initiated a change-over of the OPCN database to an IAWA-conformal database. Although the software continues to evolve, the resulting online multiple-keyed entry database is functional and accessible over the internet at http://insidewood.lib.ncsu.edu/search/. Microphotographs of specimens in this database are continually added and in 2008 a new update was released, making it more user-friendly and including a fossil wood database.

For checking possible matches, several published photographic atlases of wood anatomy are available. One of the best is the CSIRO Atlas of Hardwoods (Ilic, 1991). Others are by Kribs (1959), Miles (1978), Detienne and Jacquet (1983), Sosef, Hong & Prawirohatmodjo (1998), as well as the online photographic database of the National Herbarium Nederland (http://145.18.162.53:81/c8). The NCSU Insidewood database also has a nice bibliography attached to most listings.

Finally, the last step is to confirm identifications using research wood collections. This will be performed using the xylarium collections at the Forest Products Laboratory in Madison, Wisconsin (Madison Collection [MADw] and Samuel J. Record Collection [SJRw]), thanks to a standing invitation by Alex Wiedenhoeft, botanist at the FPL's Center for Wood Anatomy Research.

Identifications to date involve the following families:

Dicots: Alangiaceae Apocynaceae Euphorbiaceae Flacoutiaceae Juglandaceae Leguminosae Malpighiaceae Olacaceae Fagaceae (Oligocene and Miocene only) Ulmaceae (Oligocene and Miocene only)   Monocots: Palmae Gymnosperms: Araucariaceae (Cretaceous only) Cherolepidiaceae (Cretaceous only) Cupressaceae Taxodiaceae Pteridophyta (ferns): Cyathea (Eocene only) Cycadophyta: Unidentified Cycadales.

A microscopic image of a fractured fossil wood specimen from the Karnes County area. Fracture-fill is a clear to white chalcedony agate with an enclosed band of orange agate. The wood is a dicot, but cell structure is unrecognizable due to extreme silicification. Magnification about 6×. (Image from "Polygonal Fracturing in South Texas Petrified Wood"; *Rocks and Minerals*, v. 83, #2, pg. 162-165.)

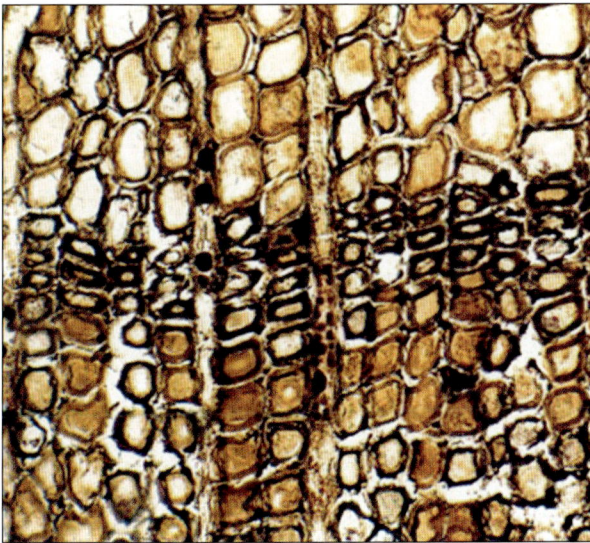

Taxodiaceae cross-section from the Jewett Lignite Mine in East-Central Texas. Magnification is 40x. Tracheids (the primary cell type present) are heavily lignitized (carbonized). The occasional black-filled cells are parenchyma. Rays appear as stripes that traverse the section from top to bottom.

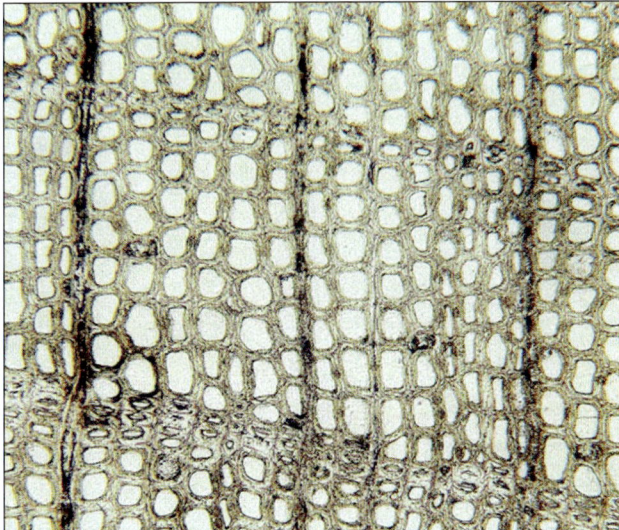

Taxodiaceae cross-section from the mid-Eocene Yegua Fm. Magnification is 79x. Annual growth rings occur at close intervals (a width of about 10 tracheids) and are abrupt (i.e., have 1-3 rows of flattened late wood tracheids that look distinctly different than the typical early wood tracheids).

APPENDIX D

The following is excerpted from Scott Singleton's *Anatomy of Fossil Woods and Paleoclimate in the Texas Gulf Coast Tertiary and Cretaceous: An Ongoing Research Project. Part 3. Other Corroborative Lines of Research* (the study in its entirety is at www.sas.org, *The Citizen Scientist*).

Abstract:

This document details the scope and procedures in an ongoing study to document fossil woods in the Texas Gulf Coast Cretaceous and Tertiary. While the first objective of the study is to identify these fossil woods, perhaps an equally important goal is to infer paleoclimate from these results. The primary methods for achieving this goal are (1) comparisons of fossil tree assemblages to modern day forest assemblages, (2) dendrochronological and dendroecological analysis of growth rings in the fossil woods, (3) sporomorph analysis of pollen and spores at fossil sites and the integration of that data with fossil wood identifications, and (4) analysis of fossil leaves either associated with the fossil woods or in nearby sediments and integrating that data with the fossil wood identifications.

Currently, work is proceeding on the first phase of this research; namely, collection, preparation, and analysis of fossil woods within the study area. This work has been ongoing since 2000 and currently involves over 700 thin section slides with about 25-100 being added per year. Sampling within the study area is very good, totaling about 100 localities.

Dendrochronology, palynology, and leaf paleobotany will each be handled as separate phases of the study.

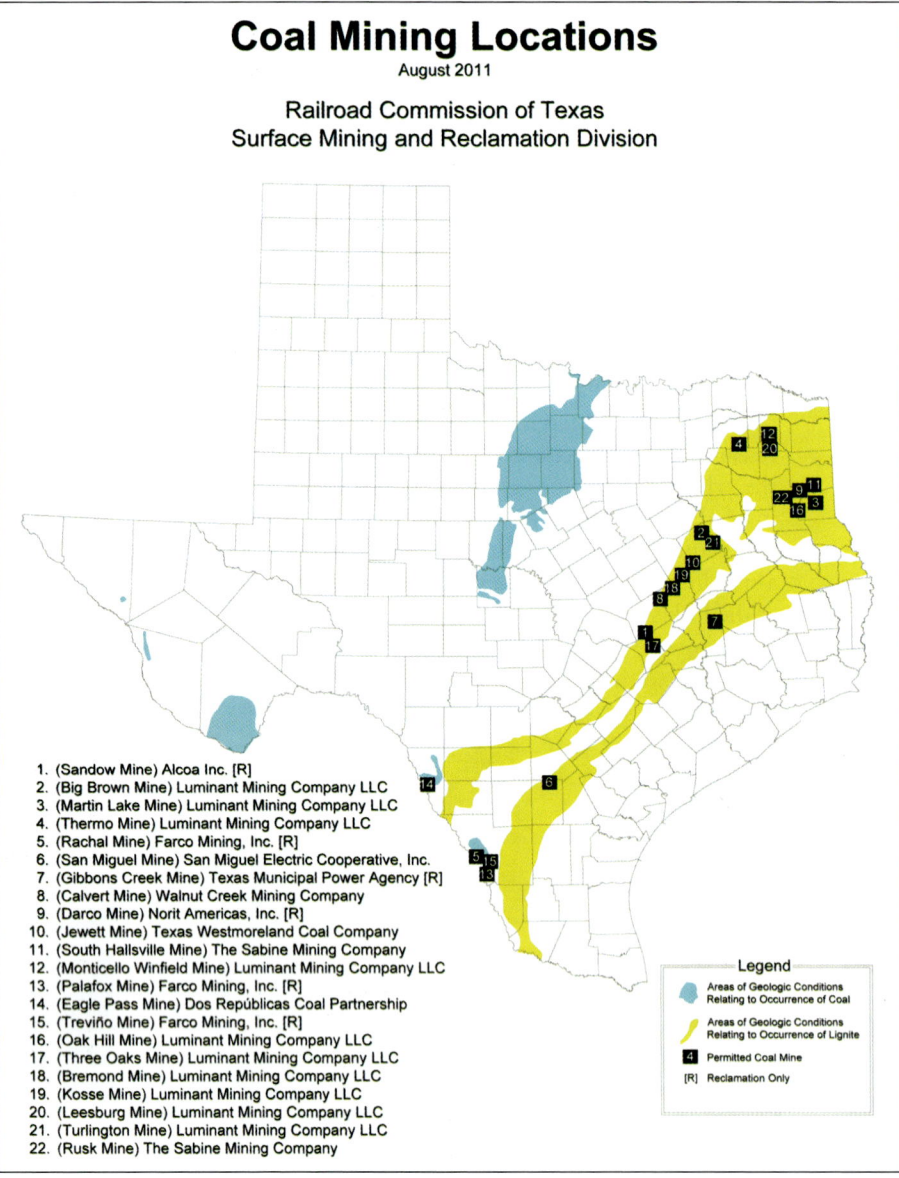

Figure 11. Lignite mines in Texas. The landward yellow strip represents the Late Paleocene/Early Eocene Calvert Bluff Formation of the Wilcox Group. The seaward yellow strip represents the Late Eocene Jackson Group. (Source: Railroad Commission of Texas, http://www.rrc.state.tx.us/forms/forms/smrd/TxCoaLst.pdf).

Analysis of Areal and Temporal Distribution, Paleoclimate

The number of specimens within most localities is, on average, sufficient to construct a reasonably diverse macrofossil assemblage, considering the inherent difficulties involved in the fossilization of organic material. Typically, most localities shown in the Texas Fossil Wood Localities map (pg. x) have between 20-70 specimens. However, the standard deviation is quite large, with a minimum of about 5-10 and a maximum of about 200-400. Considering that average species per locality are about 5-8 for small sampling populations and about 8-15 for large sampling populations, I consider 20-30 specimens to be the minimum sample size to get an idea of preserved macrofossil species variability at a site. However, I prefer sample numbers on the order of 50-100, and most of the data points I consider to be high quality fall in this range or above.

Sampling of most wood-containing stratigraphic formations is currently sufficient for both temporal and areal plant assemblage analysis.

Temporal plant analysis involves defining the change in the fossil assemblage through the Eocene, Oligocene, and Miocene in specific geographic areas. The spatial data coverage in the map on page x suggests that this is currently possible in east and central Texas. My investigations along this line have already led to the observations discussed previously in Tertiary Climatology.

Areal plant analysis defines the change in the fossil assemblage within a formation between the borders of Texas with Louisiana and Mexico, approximately 800 km (500 miles).Today, this traverses four distinct plant zones (northeast to southwest: Piney Woods, Post Oak Belt, Blackland Prairie, South Texas Brush Country). Therefore, the objective of this phase of research is to quantify how far back in time latitudinal zonation existed and what form it took. Unpublished research to date by the author has shown that there is a distinct assemblage change between East Texas and South Texas, with Central Texas being gradational between the two. Although wood identification is the primary objective of this research project, the analysis of paleoclimate is closely related and is a logical extension. Therefore, this analysis will be performed at the conclusion of investigation at each locality, and will be tied together stratigraphically and when enough information becomes available.

Dendrochronology and Dendroecology

Although secondary to the primary objective of this research, the analysis of tree rings can provide important information about the environment in which these trees lived. Several possibilities exist for research into dendrochronology and dendroecology:

The first is to investigate silicified Taxodiaceae logs associated with late Paleocene/early Eocene (Calvert Bluff Fm, Wilcox Group) lignite deposits. There are a number of lignite mines in Texas (see map, Fig. 11, Coal Mining Locations, preceding page), and my investigations indicate that all of the mines in the northeastern part of Texas have silicified, lignified Taxodiaceae logs. There are typically a large number of these logs in each mine, many of which reach several feet in diameter and contain prominent annual growth rings (Fig. 12, see pg. xi). In addition, several of the mines are in close proximity with one another along the strike of the Calvert Bluff Fm. (map, preceding page). This suggests the possibility of dendrochronological investigations on groups of logs from one or more lignite mines.

A second research possibility is to evaluate the ecological and climatological factors in one of a number of Eocene sites that contain sufficient numbers of whole or reasonably intact specimens that are either in-situ or haven't been transported far (Fig. 13 see pg. xi). One particular site in McMullen County of south Texas (late Eocene Manning Fm.) has an entire range of tree sizes in upright positions, indicating sudden burial of a woodland or forest.

In general, there are two challenges with any Eocene site (except for the lignite mine sites): (1) mineralization must not be excessive. This condition leads to degradation or obliteration of cell structure, whose preservation is essential to performing wood anatomy and dendroecology. (2) There must be a sufficient number of growth rings in the specimens. This condition is not always present due to the tropical nature of the climate in the Eocene of Texas. Even in the late Eocene, dicot specimens in some sites only have sporadic growth rings, and obviously they are not of an annual nature.

The third research possibility is similar to the second but overcomes restriction #2: Evaluation of ecological and climatological factors in representative Oligocene sites. The Oligocene depocenter is located in eastern Texas and western Louisiana (Fig. 2), so sites containing abundant fossil wood will occur in those areas. The Oligocene satisfies restriction #2 because of the cool-down that occurred at the transition between the late Eocene and the Oligocene (Part 1). This produced a subtropical or warm temperate environment in Texas and most species have distinct, annual growth rings.

Palynology

The standard for reconstructing paleo-plant communities is to analyze the presence and relative frequencies of sporomorph (spore and pollen) forms. Moreover, when sampling is performed at vertical intervals within a sediment column, changes in the plant community over time can be diagnosed. This is typically combined with lithology and stratigraphy to form a complete understanding of the paleoecology and environment of deposition.

The challenge proposed by this research is to coordinate the identification and evaluation of plant microfossils and macrofossils. Often these two lines of investigation are performed separately, leading to confusion in naming nomenclature. However, it is hoped that by combining the evaluation of these two fossil forms, this research can arrive at a much more robust and comprehensive paleoecological analysis of the Texas Gulf Coast Cretaceous and Tertiary.

Identification and Correlation of Fossil Leaves

Occasionally, leaf material is found in association with wood material during field collection in this research project. Other times leaves may be found nearby in other layers that are roughly time-correlative. In these cases, botanical collaboration would provide an opportunity for confirmation similar to that provided by palynology.

In addition, there is the possibility of collection at localities separate from the wood localities but within the same formations. This type of effort, while constituting separate and distinct research, can often still be combined with wood anatomy results to produce a cohesive research result.

Stratigraphy and Environment of Deposition

A vital component of the overall research project is to define the stratigraphic context of each locality. Sometimes this could be as basic as defining the specific member of the formation being sampled. Other times this would involve the analysis of the sediments encasing the fossils with the goal of defining the environment of deposition. In any case, geologic information is an important aspect of any paleontological investigation, and, as such, this information will be associated with any botanical results.

For example, one article by the author dealt specifically with research into the stratigraphic location of a prominent petrified wood occurrence, and the environment of deposition at that locality (Singleton, 2008). Another article in preparation (Wood Anatomy of a Pennsylvanian Fossil Forest, Eastland County, Texas) will contain a section on the geology of the fossil wood deposit by Dr. Tom Yancey of Texas A&M University.

Appendix E

Anatomy of Fossil Woods and Paleoclimate in the Texas Gulf Coast Tertiary and Cretaceous, References

AAPG, 1988, Correlation of stratigraphic units in North America—Gulf Coast region correlation chart: American Association of Petroleum Geologists, Tulsa, Oklahoma.

Abbott, M.L., 1986, Petrified wood from the Paleocene, Black Peaks Formation, Big Bend National Park, Texas. In P.H. Pause and R.G. Spears (eds), Geology of the Big Bend area and Solitario Dome, Texas. West Texas Geological Society 1986 Field Trip Guidebook, Publication #86-82, pp. 141-142.

Aubry, M., S. Lucas, and W.A. Berggren (eds.), 1998, Late Paleocene-Early Eocene Climatic and Biotic Events in the Marine and Terrestrial Records. Columbia University Press, New York, NY.

Ball, O.M., 1931, A contribution to the paleobotany of the Eocene of Texas. Bulletin of the Agricultural and Mechanical College of Texas, 4th series, v. 2, #5.

Berry, E.W., 1916, The Lower Eocene floras of Southeastern North America. USGS Professional Paper 91.

Berry, E.W., 1922a, The flora of the Woodbine Sand at Arthurs Bluff, Texas. USGS Professional Paper 129-G.

Berry, E.W., 1922b, Additions to the flora of the Wilcox Group. USGS Professional Paper 131-A.

Berry, E.W., 1924, The Middle and Upper Eocene floras of Southeastern North America. USGS Professional Paper 92.

Berry, E.W., 1930, Revision of the Lower Eocene Wilcox flora of the Southeastern States. USGS Professional Paper 156.

Berry, E.W., 1937, Tertiary floras of Eastern North America. The Botanical Review, v. 3, pp. 31-46.

Chadwick, M.L., 1988, Identification and geological significance of petrified wood from the Oligocene Catahoula Formation, Jasper County, Texas. M.S. Thesis, Stephen F. Austin State University, Nacogdoches, Texas.

Daghlian, C.P., W.L. Crepet, and T. Delevoryas, 1980, Investigations of Tertiary angiosperms: A new flora including Eomimosoidea plumose from the Oligocene of Eastern Texas. American Journal of Botany, v. 67(3), pp. 309-320.

Daghlian, C.P., and W.L. Crepet, 1983, Oak catkins, leaves and fruits from the Oligocene Catahoula Formation and their evolutionary significance. American Journal of Botany, v. 70(5), pp. 639-649.

Detienne, P. and P. Jacquet, 1983. Atlas d'identification des bois de l'amazonie et des regions voiseines. Centre Technique Forestier Tropical, Nogent s/Marne. 640 pp.

Dingus, W.F., and W.E. Galloway, 1990. Morphology, paleogeographic setting, and origin of the Middle Wilcox Yoakum canyon, Texas coastal plain. American Association of Petroleum Geologists Bulletin, v. 74, #7, pp. 1055-1076.

Dukes, G.H., 1961, Some Tertiary fossil woods of Louisiana and Mississippi. Ph. D. Dissertation, Louisiana State University, Lafayette, Louisiana.

Eargle, D.H., 1959, Stratigraphy of Jackson Group (Eocene), South-Central Texas. Bulletin of the American Association of Petroleum Geologists, vol. 43 (11), pp. 2623-2635.

Elsik, W.C., 1974, Characteristic Eocene palynomorphs in the Gulf Coast, USA. Palaeontographica, vol. 149, pp. 90-111.

Fisher, W.L., and J.H. McGowen, 1969, Depositional systems in Wilcox Group (Eocene) of Texas and their relation to occurrence of oil and gas. The American Association of Petroleum Geologists Bulletin, vol. 53 (1), pp. 30-54.

Frazier, D.W., 1966, Paragenesis of silica in silicified woods of the Whitsett Formation (Eocene) in Texas. M.S. Thesis, University of Houston, Houston, Texas.

Frederiksen, N.O., 1981, Middle Eocene to Early Oligocene plant communities of the Gulf Coast. In Communities of the Past, Gray, J., Boucot, A.J., and Berry, W.B.N. (eds.), Hutchinson Ross Pub. Co., Stroudsburg, PA

French, C.D., and C.J. Schenk, 2007, Map showing geology, oil and gas fields, and geologic provinces of the Gulf of Mexico region: U.S. Geological Survey Open-File Report 97-470-L, CD-ROM publication, < http://pubs.usgs.gov/of/ofr-97-470/OF97-470L >.

Galloway, W.E., P.E. Ganey-Curry, X. Li, and R.T. Buffler. 2000. Cenozoic depositional history of the Gulf of Mexico basin. American Association of Petroleum Geologists Bulletin, v.84, #11, pp. 1743-1774.

Galloway, W.E, 1982. Depositional framework of the Lower Miocene (Fleming) episode, Northwest Gulf Coast Basin. Gulf Coast Association of Geological Societies Transactions, v.35, pp. 67-74.

Galloway, W.E, 1989a. Genetic stratigraphic sequences in basin analysis I: Architecture and genesis of flooding-surface bounded depositional units. American Association of Petroleum Geologists Bulletin, v.73, #2, pp. 125-142.

Galloway, W.E, 1989b. Genetic stratigraphic sequences in basin analysis II: Application to Northwest Gulf of Mexico Cenozoic Basin. American Association of Petroleum Geologists Bulletin, v.73, #2, pp. 143-154.

Galloway, W.E., D.K. Hobday, and K. Magara, 1982. Frio Formation of Texas Gulf coastal plain: Depositional systems, structural framework, and hydrocarbon distribution. American Association of Petroleum Geologists Bulletin, v.66, #6, pp. 649-688.

Gennett, J.A., 1996, Comparative palynology of clastics and lignites from the Manning Formation, Jackson Group, Upper Eocene, Grimes Co., TX. Transactions— Gulf Coast Association of Geological Societies, Vol XLVI, pp. 149-157.

Graham, A., 1999, Late Cretaceous and Cenezoic history of North American Vegetation. Oxford University Press, New York, NY.

Haq, B.U., J. Hardenbol, and P.R. Vail, 1987, Chronology of fluctuating sea levels since the Triassic. Science, v. 235, pp. 1156-1166.

Herendeen, P.S., and D.L. Dilcher, 1990, Fossil mimosoid legumes from the Eocene and Oligocene of Southeastern North America. Review of Palaeobotany and Palynology, v. 62, pp. 339-361.

Hoadley, R.B., 1990, Identifying Wood: Accurate results with simple tools. Taunton Press, Newtown, Conn.

Hueber, F.M., E.M.V. Nambudiri, W.D. Tidwell, and E.F. Wheeler, 1991, An Eocene fossil tree with cambial variant wood structure. Review of Palaeobotany and Palynology, v. 68, pp. 257-267.

Ilic, J., 1991, CSIRO Atlas of Hardwoods, Springer-Verlag, New York, NY.

Jones, J.G., and J.A. Gennett, 1991, Pollen and spores from the type section of the Middle Eocene Stone City Formation, Burleson Co., Texas. Transactions— Gulf Coast Association of Geological Societies, Vol XLI, pp. 348-352.

Kribs, D.A., 1959, Commercial Foreign Woods on the American Market. Dover Publications, Inc., New York, NY.

LaPasha, C.A., 1987, General Unknown Entry and Search System. North Carolina Agricultural Research Service Bulletin 474A, North Carolina State University, Raleigh, N.C.

Lehman, T.M., and E.A. Wheeler, 2001, A fossil dicotyledonous woodland/forest from the Upper Cretaceous of Big Bend National Park, Texas. Palaios, v. 16, pp. 102-108.

Manchester, S.R., 1981, Fossil history of the Juglandaceae. Ph. D. Dissertation, Indiana University, Indianapolis, Indiana.

Manchester, S.R., 1983, Fossil wood of the Engelhardieae (Juglandaceae) from the Eocene of North America: Engelhardioxylon Gen. Nov. Botanical Gazette, v. 144(1), pp. 157-163.

Matson, G.C., and E.W. Berry, 1916a, The Catahoula Sandstone and its flora. USGS Professional Paper 98-M.

Matson, G.C., and E.W. Berry, 1916b, The Pliocene Citronelle Formation of the Gulf Coastal Plain and its flora. USGS Professional Paper 98-L.

Miles, A., 1978, Photomicrographs of World Woods. Department of the Environment, Building Research

Establishment, Garston, Watford, UK.

Penhallow, D.P., 1907, Notes on fossil woods from Texas. Transactions of the Royal Society of Canada, Section IV, vi, pp. 93-113.

Prothero, D.R., and W.A. Berggren (eds.), 1992, Eocene-Oligocene Climatic and Biotic Evolution. Princeton University Press, Princeton, NJ.

Raymond, A., M.K. Phillips, J.A. Gennett, and P.A. Comet, 1997, Palynology and paleoecology of lignites from the Manning Formation (Jackson Group) outcrop in the Lake Somerville spillway of east-central Texas. International Journal of Coal Geology, vol. 34, pp. 195-223.

Rohr, D.M., A.J. Boucot, J. Miller, and M. Abbott, 1986, Oldest termite nest from the Upper Cretaceous of West Texas. Geology, v. 14, pp. 87-88.

Singleton, S.W., 2008. Petrified wood in the Miocene Fleming Formation, Jasper County, Texas. Gulf Coast Association of Geological Societies Transactions, v. 58, pp. 797-814.

Sosef, M.S.M., L.T. Hong, & S. Prawirohatmodjo (eds.). 1998. Plant Resources of South-East Asia. No. 5 (3). Timber trees: Lesser-known timbers. Backhuys Publishers, Leiden. 859 pp.

TNRIS (Texas Natural Resources Information System), 2006, Geologic atlas of Texas: Austin, DVD-ROM publication.

Warwick, P.D., and S.S. Crowley, 1995, Coal geology of the Paleocene-Eocene Calvert Bluff Formation (Wilcox Group) and the Eocene Manning Formation (Jackson Group) in east-central Texas. USGS Open File Report 95-595.

Wheeler, E.A., and T.M. Lehman, 2000, Late Cretaceous woody dicots from the Aguaja and Javelina Fms., Big Bend National Park, Texas, USA. IAWA Journal, v. 21, pp. 83-120.

Wheeler, E.A., and T.M. Lehman, 1994, Javelinoxylon, a new genus of malvalean tree from the Upper Cretaceous of Big Bend National Park, Texas. American Journal of Botany, v. 81(6), pp. 703-710.

Wheeler, E.A., and T.M. Lehman, 2005, Upper Cretaceous—Paleocene conifer woods from Big Bend National Park, Texas. Paleogeography, Palaeoclimatology, Palaeoecology, v. 226, pp. 233-258.

Wheeler, E.A., R.G. Pearson, C.A. LaPasha, T. Zack, and W. Hatley, 1986, Computer-Aided Wood Identification. North Carolina Agricultural Research Service Bulletin 474, North Carolina State University, Raleigh, N.C.

Wheeler, E.A., 1991, Paleocene dicotyledonous trees from Big Bend National Park, Texas: Variability in wood types common in the Late Cretaceous and Early Tertiary, and ecological inferences. American Journal of Botany, v. 78(5), pp. 658-671.

Yancey, T.E., 1997, Depositional environments of Late Eocene lignite-bearing strata, east-central Texas. International Journal of Coal Geology, vol. 34, pp. 261-275.

Yancey, T.E., W.C. Elsik, and R.H. Sancay, 2003, The palynological record of Late Eocene climate change, Northwest Gulf of Mexico. In "From Greenhouse to Icehouse, the Marine Eocene-Oligocene Transition", Prother, Ivany & Nesbitt (eds.), Columbia University Press.

Publications:

Singleton, S., 2006, Cycad Anatomy and Fossil Occurrences in Texas; Fossil News, v. 12, #9, p. 4-9.

Singleton, S., 2008, Polygonal Fracturing in South Texas Petrified Wood; Rocks and Minerals, v. 83, #2, p. 162-165.

Singleton, S.W., 2008, Petrified Wood in the Miocene Fleming Formation, Jasper County, Texas; Gulf Coast Association of Geological Societies Transactions, v. 58, p. 797-814.

Singleton, S., 2009, Anatomy of Fossil Woods and Paleoclimate in the Texas Gulf Coast Tertiary and Cretaceous: An Ongoing Research Project, Part 1; The Citizen Scientist, Aug. 2009, http://www.sas.org/tcs/weekly Issues_2009/2009-08-07/feature1/index.html

Singleton, S., 2009, Anatomy of Fossil Woods and Paleoclimate in the Texas Gulf Coast Tertiary and Cretaceous: An Ongoing Research Project, Part 2; The Citizen Scientist, Sept. 2009, http://www.sas.org/tcs/weekly Issues_2009/2009-09-04/feature1/index.html

Singleton, S., 2009, Anatomy of Fossil Woods and Paleoclimate in the Texas Gulf Coast Tertiary and Cretaceous: An Ongoing Research Project, Part 3; The Citizen Scientist, Oct. 2009, http://www.sas.org/tcs/weekly Issues_2009/2009-10-02/feature1/index.html

Singleton, S.W., 2011, Dadoxylon Logs from a Late Pennsylvanian Fossil Forest, Central Texas; in review.

Appendix F

Specifications: The Hart Shoemaker House

SPECIFICATIONS

FOR A ONE STORY ROCK VENEER RESIDENCE AND GARAGE

LOCATION   RIVER SIDE DRIVE

ABILENE - TEXAS

For

Mr. and Mrs. Hart Shoemaker

---o---

These specifications are intended to embrace all labor and material necessary to the erection of this residence and garage, same to be shown on accompanying plans and described in these specifications.

EXCAVATION - FILLING AND GRADING

WORK INCLUDED:

Do all necessary excavating for all dirt and rock for all foundations and footings, sidewalks, cement floors, etc. All to be of size and depth as indicated on the drawings. The bottom of all excavations are to be levelled off ready for concrete. Also do all filling and tamping as shown and required on plans. The size of excavations for all concrete footings, etc., shall be exact size of concrete, neatly trimmed and squared up and all loose dirt removed shall be placed as directed for filling and grading around residence to secure with a uniform gradient with drainage away from buildings. Gravel floor in garage and driveway to be four inches thick and well rolled till thoroughly compacted. Any depressions which develop from rolling are to be filled with gravel and again rolled until a uniform surface is obtained.

CONCRETE AND REINFORCED CONCRETE:

The work under this heading will include the frunishing and placing of all materials, form work, rods, runways, mixing apparatus, labor, etc., necessary to construct and complete in a good substantial and workmanlike manner. All plain and reinforced concrete walls, footings, piers, cement floors, sidewalks, etc., and all work shown on the drawings as concrete or reinforced concrete either by notes or hatching, together with all cement finished noted on the drawings or called for herein.

CEMENT:

The cement used in the work shall be an approved brand of Standard Portland Cement, meeting all the requirements of the A.S.T.M. All cement shall be kept dry and fresh at all times during the process of construction of this job.

SAND AND GRAVEL

FINE AGGREGATE:

Pit run sand shall be clean and a mixture of coarse and fine grains with a coarse grain predominating. It shall be free from clay, loam, mud, sticks, organic matter or other impurities and shall be screened unless in the opinion of the supervising architect, the proportions of particles above one-fourth inch is so small that the sand will perform its functions in the concrete without screening. The sand may contain as much as three percent silt by decantations. Sand must pass the colorimetric test. At least fifteen percent shall pass a #8 screen. Contractor shall furnish screen and analysis at his expense.

COARSE AGGREGATE:

The coarse aggregate shall consist of clean pit run, hard gravel free from all impervious materials. Aggregate containing soft, flat or elongated particles shall not be used. A graduation of sizes in particles is preferred. The aggregate shall be of a size to pass through a 1-1/2 inch ring and retained on a screen having 1/4 inch dia. holes. Screen and analysis shall be the same as specified for sand and furnished by the contractor at his expense.

PROPORTIONS:

All concrete not otherwise specifically mentioned, shall be composed of one part of cement to six parts of mixed dry and rodded fine and coarse aggregate, the actual field mix will be determined after the pit run mixed sand and gravel aggregate have been approved by the supervising architect.

MIXING:

All concrete shall be machine mixed, the product delivered from the mixer shall be of the specified proportions and thoroughly mixed. Concrete shall be mixed, using just sufficient water to make a mass of such consistency that the reinforcing steel will become covered, while at the same time care must be taken to avoid an excess of water so as not to cause a separation of the ingredients. The amount of water used shall not exceed six gallons to one sack of cement including the water in the aggregate. The maximum slump of concrete shall be six inches.

PLACING CONCRETE:

After the mixing of concrete as specified, it shall be transported to the point of construction and placed in the forms without delay. When the concrete has been deposited in forms it shall be thoroughly puddled and exposed surfaces worked so that a smooth finish will result. Before placing any concrete, care must be taken that the space to be occupied by concrete is free from debris, that the forms are well wetted and the reinforcing bars are kept in their correct positions.

WETTING:

The surfaces of concrete exposed to premature drying shall be kept damp by thoroughly sprinkling for a period of seven days to prevent possible checking from too rapid hardening.

JOINTS IN CONCRETE:

Should it become necessary to stop concreting, the joint shall be made by means of bulkheads. All bulkheads shall be provided with a triangular strip to form a 2" x 2" key in the center of same, and shall be so placed as to positively prevent the loss of any of the ingredients of the concrete. Bulkheads shall not be removed until the concrete has set hard and before concreting is resumed all debris shall be removed from the form adjacent to the bulkheads so as to form a close, neat joint. In no case shall a bulkhead be placed in the center of a beam but must come over the center of a pier or in a wall where there is a continuous footing.

WATER:

The owner shall furnish all water required and pay the city authorities for same.

REINFORCEMENTS:

The reinforcing bars for walls, footings, etc., shall be of an approved type having a positive mechanical bond with the concrete and shall be rail concrete reinforcement rods manufactured by the open hearth or Bessemer process. In general, the reinforcement shall be assembled in the forms in such a manner and so wired or fastened, that it will be definitely and rigidly held in place during the concreting. The size and spacing of the bars and their arrangement, are carefully shown on the plans, except the following, tie all concrete steps to concrete floors or walls as the case may be, with three 3/8" round rods, the length of stair stringers spacing one 2" in from each edge and one in the center. Place one 3/8" rod the length of step just below each stair riser. Keep the reforcing rods 1-1/2" above the earth, which is to be in all cases well packed and tamped even and smooth.

FORMS:

For concrete walls and piers, build forms of one inch or two inch stuff, dressed to a uniform thickness. Forms are to be put together in such a manner that they may be easily removed without jarring the concrete. The lumber to be assembled with reasonably tight joints properly laid, to prevent any part of the concrete leaking through or leaving objectionable variations between joints in surface of boards. All forms and centering shall be kept in place with braces, shores, anchors, wire, bolts, etc., to avoid undue bulging on account of concrete while placing same. Be sure that all foundation walls are level, keeping garage wall 8-3/4" above residence wall.

CEMENT FLOORS AND SIDEWALKS:

Construct all concrete floors, sidewalks, steps, and splash blocks, same size and location as indicated on drawings. Lay all walks in 4 ft. sections and joint. Top of all these surfaces to be straight edged off while concrete is wet and it shall be sprinkled uniformally with a mixture of Portland Cement and sharp sand in proportions of one part of Cement to one part of sand mixed dry over the surface to absorb the surplus water, then same shall be floated into the concrete with heavy wooden floats and trowelled smooth with steel trowel. Front porch, terrace and steps, to have 3/4" topping composed of one part cement to two parts sand, with best grade of red coloring well mixed to insure uniform color throughout.

FLOOR HARDENING

Concrete contractor will treat porch, terrace and garage floors with 3 coats of Lapidolith or Vitrufyl or equal floor hardener, applied in strict accordance with the manufacturer's directions.

ROCK:

The owner will furnish all hard rocks and field stone at the job site. The rock and field stone consist of irregular shaped pieces approximately 12" x 15" and have a general uniform thickness of approximately 5 inches. The pieces of rock are in various colors and the owner will stipulate to the rock contractor as to how he wishes to have the percentage of various colors distributed throughout the walls. The rock contractor will exercise care in choosing the pieces of rock and in placing same in wall. He will consult with the owner and show sample of work on both beaded and raked joints, that the owner may make a preference. Before the rock contractor commences his work, he shall inspect the building walls to be sure that they are plumb and in line, with all sheathing in place and covered completely with waterproof building paper which shall extend down and under the bottom course of veneer. Any exception he may find he shall report to the general contractor to have properly fixed before proceeding with his work.

Lay all rock and stone in a full bed of mortar composed of 2-1/2 parts of sand to one part of cement. All joints throughout must be thoroughly and effectually filled with mortar. All rock shall be wetted down before being laid into the wall. Use flexible noncorrodible metal ties 3/4" x 7" to anchor rock veneer to frame. Spacing of ties to be ever 18" vertically and every 24" horizontally, driving nails where studs occur, where possible. No retempering of mortar will be permitted. Keep face of all wall surfaces reasonably smooth, plumb and straight in line. All corners of building and col's, etc., must be plumb and show straight lines. Construct all col's, walls, arches, window headers, etc., of solid rock as specified and shown on plans. Be sure all steel lintels are in their proper place over all openings and resting 6" on masonry at each end of opening. Rock mason will cooperate with roof and metal contractor to insure a good job of flashing where same occurs at chimney and side walls. Clean down all walls at the completion of the rock work.

STEEL LINTELS:

Furnish and install 4" x 4" steel lintels over all square openings of exterior mason walls, to rest six inches on all rock revealed. Lintels over garage doors to run full length over both doors.

TERRACE RAILINGS:

Owner will furnish iron railings and deliver same to job for setting. Rock contractor will cooperate with carpenter contractor. The latter will set 1" pipe nipples 6", one in rock wall of house, and one in rock col. 2 ft. and 9" above terrace floor as shown on plans. Carpenter contractor will also furnish and install 3/4" x 6" nipples in floor of terrace where shown on plans.

STONE TRIM:

Furnish and install lueders natural limestone window sills cut to length from stock size 5" x 7". All single window sills to be in one piece. All double windows not over two pieces to sill. All sills to be handled carefully and set in place in first class condition, level, smooth and in line. All stone trim for arches, col's, window headers, etc., to be of natural rock and cut on job as necessary to execute design of shape and strength.

AIR VENTS AND LOUVERS:

Furnish and install 13 - 6" x 12" cast iron Grilles as shown and located on plans. Also furnish and install 5 louvers in accordance with specifications and details shown on plans. Contractor will make 13 boards of size necessary to close openings of grilles during cold weather. Same to be painted.

TERMITE PREVENTION:

Termite shields with not less than 28 ga. G. I. shall be installed in a manner acceptable to the government F. H. A. These shields shall be continuous and shall have tight seams or soldered joints. They shall be installed on top of all foundation walls and piers and around all pipes or cut-offs in contact with the ground and extending up into the first floor framing.

Appendix G

Tom Garrett, Stonemason
Stone Cutting and Masonry- By Jim Law

Tom Garrett, a native of Albany, followed in his father's footsteps, as did his two brothers. John Garrett was a stone mason.

In 1922 Tom began the four-year apprenticeship to become a certified stone mason. One of his first projects was helping to build the west wing of the old school. In 1924 he returned to work on the east wing. It was after Tom had acquired his certification that he built the Albany High School gym in 1926 and 1927.

Mr. Garrett's masonry can be seen on many churches in both Albany and Breckenridge. In Albany this includes the annex on the Presbyterian Church, the Christian Church and Church of Christ. He worked on the Methodist Churches in both Albany and Breckenridge.

Many Albany homes, old and new, were built by Tom Garrett -- John Musselman's ranch house, and the homes of R.C. Daniel, Billy Ayers, Clarence Waller, Bill Couger, J. Dickie, C. C. Mormon, and Harold Law.

As I watched Mr. Garrett work on one of Albany's future businesses, the "Fort Griffin Mercantile," I began to realize what

All pictures in this article are buildings that Mr. Garrett has built. This is the Methodist Church Annex built in ~~1930~~ 1949.

268 • *Stone-Tree Houses of Texas*

Stonemason

it takes to be a stone mason. First of all, you have to know the characteristics of many different kinds of rock. One of the hardest rocks to cut is native limestone, while limestone from Lueders cuts the easiest. Mr. Garrett works mainly with these two kinds of limestone, and also with native sandstone.

To make mortar, Mr. Garrett uses this mixture: three parts sand to one part masonry cement. To achieve the right consistency, temperature is very important; the ingredients will not mix well unless they are over forty degrees.

Several special tools and machines are needed to cut the stone and mix the mortar. Time and experience are necessary in learning to use this equipment, especially the brick saw which trims rocks. One must manually control the rock which is placed on rollers and moved back and forth under the blade; at the same time a pedal underneath the table adjusts the height of the blade as it cuts through the stone. Less complicated tools are the hammer, chisel, and cement spatula.

On each rock building Mr. Garrett works on, the rocks have to be chosen one at a time. Out of a large pile of stones, he selects a rock close to the size and shape he needs, but even then he will have to trim it. The top of each layer of stone must be perfectly level, even though within each layer

The Billy Ayres house, formerly the Francis Taylor home.

The Harold Law home built in 1960.

the lengths of the rocks will vary. The brick saw makes the top of the rock very flat and square. However, to achieve a rounded, natural look in the wall, Mr. Garrett must chip away the sharp corners and edges of the top and bottom of the rock with a hammer and chisel. After the rock has the right shape, he lays the mortar and puts the stone into position. The space between layers of rock, filled with mortar, is called the "joint."

The complete procedure of laying each rock "in a wall" will take from 5 to 15 minutes. Laying the stone around doors, windows and electrical conduits requires much more time.

Tom Garrett has been practicing his profession of stone masonry for over fifty years. In this time, Albany has been enriched with many buildings that are as beautiful as they are lasting and solid. They are even more precious to use for the fact that no one except Tom Garrett could have made them. Unfortunately, it is doubtful that any young persons will dedicate themselves to this profession--a dying art.